D1558820

LETTERS

1949
P.E.I.
1950

FROM THE MANSE

Letters from the Manse
Joan Archibald Colborne

Island Studies Press
Charlottetown
2003

Letters from the Manse
ISBN 0-919013-39-2
© 2003 by Joan Archibald Colborne
Second printing, 2004

Manuscript preparation, proofreading: Emilie Adams
Editing: John Cousins, Laurie Brinklow
Design: UPEI Graphics
Printing: Transcontinental Prince Edward Island

Island Studies Press gratefully acknowledges the support of The Canada Council for the Arts' Emerging Publisher Program; and the Prince Edward Island Department of Community and Cultural Affairs' Cultural Development Program.

National Library of Canada Cataloguing in Publication

Colborne, Joan Archibald, 1922–
    Letters from the Manse / Joan Archibald Colborne.

ISBN 0-919013-39-2

        1. Colborne, Joan Archibald, 1922– —Correspondence.
2. Spouses of clergy—Prince Edward Island—Biography. 3. United Church of Canada—Prince Edward Island—Biography. I. Title.

BX9883.C65A3 2003   287.9'2'092   C2003-902908-5

Island Studies Press
University of Prince Edward Island
Charlottetown, PE Canada C1A 4P3
www.islandstudies.com

In memory of Blair
and in gratitude to
all the Island people
who were generous
and helpful to us
so long ago.

CONTENTS

or not, because I did an unforgiveable thing which rat
"tone" of our bath hour - namely, I got soap in his ey
hurt, and <u>mad</u>, he screamed and yelled and roared. To
try again. And tomorrow I will remember that the outle
water should be hung up on a little hook provided for
I won't have a huge puddle on the floor when the bath

Michael got another present this week. The Bethe
gave him dear little silver mug with "Michael"(anyway,
graved on it. That was very nice of them, and it makes
them for suddenly calling on me for a "few Words" the
went to.

Friday was a great day for me - I left my husband
and I went to town. The Collicutts were going and so I
ortunity to go along as I had been thinking about getti
doctor. I have had two ailments, which while not serio
cramped my style. The first was my tongue! I had funn
on it and for a day or so I couldn't eat and I couldn't
but life was dull! Dr. Dewar gave me some stuff for it
I feel like a normal tongued creature. Then I had a gr
on the first finger of my right hand, an infection from
guessed it - jabbing myself with a safety pin. I was l
The Doctor told me I had just missed having a thing cal
around" in which the infection runs around the nail and
to have your nail removed. But mine didn't run around
he lanced it and today it is all gone. I had a wonderf
town, I shopped at the drug store, the meat store, the
and the department store and I went to the bank and I s
got news, and I saw a house being moved by twelve horse
little bit of time at the Dicksons, they are all well.
nice change, and I came home to find my husband with hi
up doing dishes - he had prepared formula for Michael a
bottle and Michael was very full and very happy and <u>soa</u>
said that he felt him before he fed him and decided tha
without changing until I got home.

We are once more avid radio fans, and I give thank
BC, it has such wonderful programs of all types. It t
or which Canadians can be very proud. I wonder if you
ew Sunday Evening Hour, a religious period from 8 to 8.
he best thing in religious broadcasting I have heard.
ttawa.

Blair has just come in from church very elated, he
cheque which means we are completely paid up for 1949,
reached a <u>good</u> sermon. It was really good too, I read
s the result of the study/cleaning operation, he can f
t is more satisfactory to write a sermon at a desk than
able.

This is enough for tonight - for a

Introduction

Introduction

There was a time, no further away than half a century, when Canadians were mainly a country people, scattered in a network of village and farming communities, to the edges of Canada. And though fifty years is a short time, we have largely forgotten that vast and viable rural world with its commonplace trademarks: the farms, the schools, the stores, the repair shops. And, in thousands of these places, seeking to give spiritual unity to the ordinary people, laboured the Protestant clergyman and his wife. For the church was centred, physically and spiritually, in the daily life of the people.

They were a special breed, these churchmen and women. We knew them from a distance, for they were in our place, but somehow not of it. We knew they were special and important and otherworldly. They did not think or feel like the rest of us, and if they experienced the pleasant joys and pastimes that we knew, we did not see it. If we knew their first names, we dared not use them. If they had a sense of humour, no one heard it. It was common knowledge that they had little or no sex life, and, if they had children, they were children somehow set apart. They were not demonstrative, as nearly as we could tell. They did not attend dances nor did they discuss hockey. They had apparently no knowledge of the fight at the party down the road. Infuriatingly to all parties involved, they did not take sides in disputes between neighbours. They did not Gossip, and They Did Not Take the Name of The Lord Their God in Vain. Some of them (the men) smoked, but most did not, and, surely, They Did Not Drink. Most important of all, They Did Not Talk Politics, though their very innocuous reference was analyzed by parishioners who pondered their allegiances. Their toil, we believed, was useful, but if pressed we could not really tell what they did during the six days of the week that were not Sabbath (not that we took much time to think about it). Apparently they visited the sick, and sometimes the healthy, and they probably wrote a lot because we knew that some of them composed their sermons beforehand. Some of them spoke well from the pulpit, and, if they didn't, we did not hold it against them.

But we never questioned the fact that we needed them badly, for, if there was a haven of rest beyond this world, they held the key to it. As children we did not know what adults knew: that we needed them most when Sorrow came. And thank the Lord that children do not know the power of sorrow in the way that grown-ups do. Ministers and their partners gave grown-ups permission to mourn and to cry, which, when we grew up, we found to be a good thing.

We knew also that Protestant clergy usually came in pairs, and that, too, was good, since it was generally believed that the manse was built for at least two people. To have one person rattling around in that big house, whatever its condition, was a shame. And everyone agreed that the Minister's job was so important that it was hard to do it properly without a lifelong partner. Thus, The United Church Couple.

Of course, we know now that our views of them were wrong, and that our picture was painted only in stark black and white. We know that a myriad of brilliant colours were there if only they were painted in. But the voices of the Couples are strangely muted, and we look in vain for a good description of what they thought of us, of themselves, of the immensely important work they did, and of the countryside in which they laboured. This omission is not unimportant, for, as I said earlier, they covered this country at a time of great change, and they exerted an immense positive force in rural Canada. Nor is the omission surprising, for the past is the country of untold stories. And besides, in their dedication—almost obsession—to serve, they were the consummate professionals. To talk "outside" about delicate and sensitive and heartbreaking work was to compromise precious success. And They Did Not Compromise.

Hence the importance of Joan Colborne's wonderful *Letters from the Manse*. For she paints in the vivid colours we knew were there, and illuminates the fascinating personal experience of two young, idealistic, and dynamic church people in rural Canada of half a century ago. And, just as important, the letters speak with a universality that gives voice to the rest of the Church Couples from those times. Her accounts are so wonderfully irreverent, so human, so young at heart, so infused with idealism and hope, and so true. Those of us, in our hundreds of thousands who remember those lost days, those of us whose lives were touched by their work, will read these and say: "This is what I hoped and expected they were like. Now I know it."

To their story: a few months before they were married, Blair got his first posting, as minister of three churches in Prince Edward Island. It was the dead of winter, January 1949. The newlyweds landed in a world in which, city-bred as they were, they had little experience. Blair's first charge was the churches of three hamlets stretched over fifteen miles of the Island's northwest coast. To the north, along the shore facing

New Brunswick, lay Cape Wolfe, a farming and fishing village. Six miles south of Cape Wolfe and a couple miles inland was the community of Springfield West, the centre of the pastoral charge with Bethel United Church and manse. South of the manse, about eight miles by road, lay the community of Glenwood.

Depending on the particular hamlet, English and Scots pioneers had settled this area between 1805 and 1850, with the majority coming between 1820 and 1840. Eventually, the coastal communities had expanded inland, creating farming settlements such as Springfield West. The parishioners—farming and fishing people—were no richer or poorer than most other rural Canadians, notwithstanding the fact that the average wage on PEI at that time was about half that of the rest of Canada.

In the summertime, a half-century ago, this spot was as pleasant a place as you could wish to be. The red clay roads bordered small, gently rolling hedgerowed fields to the edge of the Capes. In the spring, long windrows of young people ambled slowly down the fields, dropping potato sets. At haying time, clover scented the air, for this was good land, light and warm. At harvest time came the rattle of binders, with men behind them stooking. And, in the fall, when you bent over your potato basket, the sound you heard was the heavy clank of harness when the horses snapped into their work pulling the potato diggers.

But in January 1949, winter told another tale. By then, the warm westerlies had turned to freezing gales, and small children arrived home from school crying from the aching cold in their faces, and big tough boys sometimes walked backwards into the bitter wind so their noses and ears wouldn't freeze. And in the snow months between December and March, the woodstoves could not keep the frost from the windowpanes, even in the middle of the day. The driving wind turned white with the snow it carried, and hedgerows bowed to the east under the blasts. This was PEI writ large, and rural Canada writ small—a place of no paved roads or electricity, where snowploughs and bathrooms were a rarity, but weeklong blizzards were not.

Five days after they arrived, on January 12, 1949, Joan began her account of life at the Bethel manse at Springfield West. The manse was cold and rat-infested. Pipes and drains froze, water pumps stuck. Unlike the vast majority of houses in the community, there was a bathroom, albeit one so dysfunctional that Joan began to envy the ordinary farming people with their "wee hoose" or outside toilet. Car travel was simply impossible, and was more trouble than it was worth. Soon they resorted to the horse and sleigh, which we mistakenly connect with earlier times. And later, Blair walked, many miles across country, to one of his churches, and to visit the sick. In many a real way, this could have been 1849.

Somehow, in the euphoria of married life, Joan managed to find time to ignore it all: the physical hardships, the out-of-sync feelings, and the culture shock. On Sunday afternoons, while Blair preached in one of the three churches, she forgot the rats, the cold, and "that Goddamned Water System," armed herself "with an old portable typewriter," and wrote to her family. The preponderant ambience of the letters is of love, humour, and enjoyment of life and work. We see through her eyes the essential goodness and generosity of country people in hard times. Some of her best vignettes are of rural social life: the entertainment in "little stuffy" country halls; of weddings where the practice of the chiveree and "bouncing" were still common. She writes about the eternal waxing and waning of the seasons, the winter storms that came like a slap in the face, and the sudden coming of spring. She writes about the birth of Michael, their first child, and the inevitable storm that followed. Her images of country scenes, gone now, are so close to the heart's core that they are sad for those who remember them.

These are telling episodes of things which we ought to know, but have forgotten. This was a time when rural Canada counted for something, when F. R. Scott, a major Canadian poet and National President of the CCF Party of Canada, would sit in a rural manse and type out his O'Leary speech on Joan's old typewriter. (Blair, still remembered as a great CCF supporter, had broken the commandment that rural ministers Did Not Talk Politics.)

These true and vivid accounts are an invaluable legacy. Joan Colborne made us remember what it was like to live at a time when neighbours would refuse to leave the community for fear that the clergyman might get himself in trouble and not be able to get to church. Or when a minister would walk eight miles to see a sick member of the congregation, through drifts that a horse could not travel through. Or three miles through the woods to preach. And we realize it is not that long ago when a minister's wife "blushed crimson" because someone from the charge might have seen her looking at baby clothes. Or when a little boy, seeing Blair taking washing from the clothesline, would tell his older sister, "My, the minister sure is good to his woman." They are wonderfully poignant and true pictures of where we come from—evoking a world of battery radios, the smell of oil lamps, sleigh rides, and telephone party lines.

She writes about the work of a church which was a dynamic force in the changes the country was undergoing as it modernized. Her experience was both an Island and a Canadian reality. Islanders and, indeed, all people who remember their roots in rural Canada will recognize Joan's story. Joan and Blair Colborne spent three years in the community, and even though it is more than half a century ago, they are still remembered by the older people.

An African proverb says that a river that forgets its source will dry up. Closer to home, Milton Acorn, the great Island poet, said it another way in his poem "The Squall." He writes of life's oddity that in a sea of storms, men and women look backwards as they row their boat to safety, "Taking direction from where they'd been / With only quick-snatched glances at where they're going."

Joan Colborne's letters make sure our rivers of memory will not dry up, and from them we know that if we are to reach our destination, sometimes we have to look back.

John Cousins

_____

John Cousins is an historian and folklorist who was seven years old when the Colbornes came to live in Springfield West. He and his family lived in the next community over.

Prologue

First, I must do what all good Islanders do: tell you about my family. Blair Colborne was born in Sydney, Nova Scotia, in 1924. His father, Albert Blair (known as "A. B."), operated a large grocery store in Sydney, at the corner of Argyle and Wentworth Streets, next to Wentworth Park. His mother was Florence Matheson, also from Sydney. He had one younger brother, Edward. Blair graduated from Sydney Academy. On graduation he attended Dalhousie University and Pine Hill Divinity Hall in Halifax, where he graduated and was ordained to the ministry of the United Church of Canada in 1948. During the summers he worked at the Sydney steel plant and preached on mission fields in Saskatchewan and Alberta.

I was Joan Archibald. I was born in Halifax. My father was Maynard B. Archibald, son of a farmer from Manganese Mines, Colchester Co. (pop 64). He spent most of his youth in Truro and went to school there. He went overseas during the First World War, then went to Dalhousie and became a lawyer and then a judge. My mother was Helen Dustan, daughter of Rev. John Dustan, a Presbyterian minister. She was a descendant of Rev. James MacGregor, a pioneer clergyman in the Maritimes. She was a secretary. When I graduated from Dalhousie I went to the United Church Training School in Toronto, where deaconesses and missionaries and workers in religious education were trained. I worked as General Secretary in the Student Christian Movement at the University of Saskatchewan in Saskatoon for two years—then I went to Sarnia, Ontario, and worked as a lay minister in a new little church built at the end of the war.

On December 30, 1948, I married the Rev. Blair Colborne in Chalmers United Church in Ottawa. I was twenty-six; Blair was twenty-four.

We were well-educated, intelligent city-dwellers with high ideals and expectations. But city-dwellers we were, and when we arrived in Prince Edward Island at the beginning of January 1949, we had no idea what lay ahead of us. We were sent to a little place, Springfield West, on the west end of the Island. We were seven miles by unpaved road from O'Leary. We had a rather large house with a "water system"—meaning a gasoline engine pump that the minister activated each morning while he lay on the dirt floor of the basement on his back. We were two miles from the nearest power line. And, at that time, there were only two snowploughs on the Island.

In the beginning, I faithfully wrote letters to our scattered families, typing them by lamplight on Blair's portable typewriter on Sunday afternoon while Blair preached at one of his three churches. It made a great excuse to not have to hear the same sermon three times. I made five copies on onion skin paper: one for his parents, one for his brother (Ed), one for my sister (Budge), one for my parents, and I saved copy number five for our files. This is copy number five—and it shows that Business was not my specialty.

Blair died in 1980, and I am now over eighty. When I found these letters in Blair's files, I wanted to share them with our children and grandchildren, and some close friends. It was my son David who thought they might be of interest to the wider world. I am thankful to my publisher, Laurie Brinklow, and my Editor, John Cousins, for putting our story in perspective. It is not easy to see that you are a part of historical change when you are living through it.

Finding the letters was a real thrill: I could remember every day so clearly. Apart from omitting a few lines, and cleaning up my spelling, I haven't made any changes. I even left in swear words and ashtrays — so that people could know we really were human.

We spent three very happy years on the Island. I am overwhelmed as I look back over these letters at the goodness of people. Their aid to us was tremendous. Their patience with us was neverending. I don't think we ever thanked them enough.

The Letters

Our wedding Day, Dec. 30, 1948

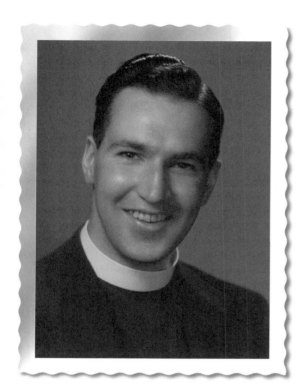

19   Joan Archibald Colborne

The Nash

Glenwood Church

The manse

Eating Lobster

Cape Wolfe Church

Blair in his aviator suit

My first and only
time on skis

The Parsonage,
O'Leary RR 1
P.E.I.
Jan. 12, 1949

Dear Folks,

This morning I looked across the breakfast table and said in senti-mental tones, "My dear, at 2.15 this afternoon we will have been mar-ried for thirteen days." To which my husband replied rather bluntly, "Thirteen, days—heavens, it seems like a century!" And there is some truth in his rather rude statement—there is nothing like coping with an unfamiliar furnace, a temperamental water system, a coal stove (when you have never cooked with anything but electricity) and a few rats, together to make a couple feel very completely married. We're thinking of writing a novel in the long winter evenings—it will be entitled, "From the Mayfair to the Manse", with subtitle, "That God-damned Water System"—if we write it this year it will be a best seller, because everyone is writing about the trials and tribulations of the private and public life of ministers right now.

This letter is my attempt to keep the Acrhibalds (see, it is so long since I have been an Archibald that I can't even remember how to spell the word) and the Colbornes both informed about the doings of this family. You will have to excuse the typing —This is an unfamiliar ma-chine to me and its spelling and grammar don't seem to be very good, and it makes a great many mistakes. And if you should happen to be the recipient of the bottom carbon copy you likely won't be able to read it anyway. However since so far we have simply not been able to find the time to write letters—please forgive us and try to put up with it.

We have now been living in the parsonage for five days, and are gradually beginning to get to rights. I have been cleaning and scrub-bing and trying to get unpacked while Blair has been nursing the fur-nace and the water system with love and care. It wasn't until nine last night that I even got the trunk with my clothes in it even opened—and our wedding presents have not arrived yet—at least they are at the sta-tion in O'Leary, but only came yesterday and we have not yet found a means of transporting them out here into the sticks. But the place is beginning to look like home. We got up all our bookends and ashtrays and a few pictures in the living room and it almost looks like a place of human habitation. This morning I scrubbed the bathroom and the bedroom and the dining room. Tomorrow—oh horrors—I must start on the kitchen and the pantry. The water system is even worse than I had expected, first of all you never know whether or not it will start at all and then when it does the belt invariably comes off the fan and the valve off the axle or something weird and then again no water. But it is making one thing very clear to me—gosh but I have a good tempered husband! —If I was the one who had to struggle with the #$%'/$ thing I just wouldn't be fit to live with. My only problems are the drain which just doesn't run out, and the fire that goes sadly out whenever I attempt to light it. All in all, we're having an awful lot of fun and a certain amount of work, and we think we're so darned lucky to have a nice house all of our own to start out our married life that we don't know what to do.

Our first Sunday on the field was a beautiful one—sunny, mild, it was impossible to believe that it was the middle of January. The eleven o'clock service was at Glenwood. We drove straight west to the shore and then along the coast. Northumberland Strait was a brilliant blue and the red earth of the Island was just as red as they tell you it is. There was almost no snow anywhere, and the roads are pretty well clear of ice. The car is running very well. Glenwood is a lovely little church—in fact I couldn't get over how very attractive all three churches are—nicer than any country churches I have seen before. I confess that I went in rather fear and trembling—you know it is a great risk to marry a preacher before you have heard him preach. But I know now that I don't have to worry about that—he's good! And it is most interesting to hear the same sermon three times and note all the variations that it picks up en route. At all three points they urged me to join the choir. I've always wanted to be in a choir, and so I think maybe I will—for this will likely be the only chance I will ever have—though it will be hard on the choirs. There were about sixty or so at church— Glenwood is the best of the three points, really a very strong little church. The first night we were here a group came up to the house and presented us with a pair of beautiful blankets and 21 dollars from the congregation and a little table from the Young People's Union and at the Women's Missionary Society yesterday that group gave us a lovely hooked rug (and it is certainly welcome—because we haven't a single rug or mat in the house. The Gorrills, where Blair boarded, invited us for dinner and then we came back to Springfield for 3.00 service (by the way we live in Springfield—I have finally found out that the place has a name and that is it). We had supper home and sat and listened to the radio until it was time to start out for the 7.30 service at Cape Wolfe. This time we went along the shore in the opposite direction. It was funny to be in the church at night with all the lamps on. This is the smallest church but somehow I liked it best. There is no greater relief to come to the last benediction on Sunday, and we drove home in the moonlight feeling like very, very free mortals. We came back and made a fire in the stove and when it had gone down had toast and jam and coffee, and felt very pleased with life.

On Monday we decided to go into Summerside, as it might be the last chance we would have before spring and there were a lot of things we needed to get. So we went in and shopped there and had lunch and shopped some more. We find there are so many things we need, especially kitchen equipment. On Friday night the Ladies Aid of Springfield is giving us a kitchen shower, and we don't want to buy anything until we see what we draw there. Until Saturday we had 1 saucepan, which we were using as kettle, coffee pot, saucepan, and casserole dish, but we got desperate and decided that we couldn't wait for the shower and bought ourselves a kettle—they're very expensive. I don't mind the lamps at all, in fact I rather like them, except that it is a pest cleaning the chimneys, and I <u>can't</u> get used to the fact that if I leave a room I have to take the light with me. I haven't tried the flatirons yet—we are living in dirt and wrinkles for the first week.

How we love to get mail! The mailman drives by just at breakfast time each morning. Unfortunately we can't see our box from the table so each morning we can't wait any longer and Blair goes down for the mail just five minutes before the mailman comes. Presents and cards are still arriving. Yesterday we received the quilt from the Schwartz's— it is a lovely one, white with blue squares, and with it were <u>four</u> cups and saucers, and in the same mail a pair of silver napkin rings from Molly. The quilt now graces the spare room bed, which is awaiting spring visitors—and the napkin rings have gone into use immediately. The Schwartz's were so good to us, for they sent a telegram as well. This morning we received a sterling silver gravy boat from Mrs. Norrie of Truro and a silver cake server from Margaret Farquhar.

Yesterday was the Annual meeting at Glenwood church with the WMS meeting at the same time, so Blair went to one and I went to the other. This was the group who were so thoughtful as to elect me their president at the December meeting. However I managed to get out of it, and am now just an ordinary member, not an office holder. We stayed out there for supper afterwards and came home to do more unpacking and clearing up. Today was the annual meeting at Cape Wolfe, and while Blair is there I am getting this written. Tonight there is to be a supper at Glenwood, and then Young Peoples there afterwards. Tomorrow annual meeting here at Springfield and in the evening Springfield Ladies Aid. Therefore so far we are not finding time hanging heavily on our hands!

This will be all on the installment from the Colbornes.

With love

Joan

To Budge

Blair is giving me a special drawer in his study for your letters - I am under strict orders not to throw any of them away! And he has never even seen an illustrated one.

And thank you so much for being such a beautiful and patient bridesmaid.

Married life is wonderful!

And P.S. : Would you mind saving this letter and returning it sometime. Blair has just read it + says that it can be chapter I of "from M. to M."

The Manse

January 18

Dear Fathers, Mothers, Brother, Sister,

I am afraid that you will fear that this family have become completely lost in the wilds of The Island, but that isn't quite true—I apologize for our dearth of correspondence, especially when you people have been so good about writing. We face two problems here when it comes to letter writing: first, finding the time to write—for there seems to have been something going on each day, and nobody ever told me how busy a housewife's life was! And secondly, getting our letters mailed. Until we get a new mailbox we either have to stand all morning at the window looking for the mail man and then dash out around the house and down our long drive way before he gets away, or else go into O'Leary to do our letter mailing. So you will see that there are problems involved. Blair's church reports have to go today so we are going into town this afternoon and therefore I will sit down in this filthy house amid piles of unwashed laundry and get a letter off to you.

As I have said, life has been very full, both with activities and domestic comedies and tragedies as well. We're learning much in these first couple of weeks. I'm learning to close doors after using, ever since a rat got into our cold room and ate our whole supply of meat. And Blair is learning to empty slop pails cheerfully (?) as our sink has completely given up the ghost. I have learned that when you serve tea to the Board of Stewards here you do not use your best china—because the farmers get so completely scared that they will break something that they can't eat. And Blair is learning to wear long woolly underwear without scratching too much. And we are learning the kindness and generosity of the country people. Hardly a day goes by but what somebody brings us something—a jar of preserves, a bottle of thick country cream, a load of kindling, people are just amazing. Blair did a good job before I came— he told everyone that he was marrying a city girl, and he didn't think she knew anything much about cooking and keeping house—the result has been that they have constantly shown how sorry they are for him by bringing us food. On Friday evening the Springfield people came here to the manse and had a shower for us, there were mobs here—we ran out of chairs and had to sit on trunks, stairs and floor. They had everything decorated with streamers and bells, and even a wedding cake with a bride and groom on top. It was very, very awkward, as showers always are. They presented us with an occasional chair and a couple of satin cushions (we are hoping that we can graciously present all three to the manse when we leave) also a kitchen clock (we'll keep that) and a cup and saucer—and many other things which they knew we needed, like a dish pan, an ironing board, an egg beater, a rolling pin, a sauce pan etc, etc. By the time the other point has a shower for us, we will be all set up for comfortable and convenient house keeping. For the reception that evening we really put on the dog, I got out my beautiful table cloth and crystal candle sticks and cups and saucers. There is still one box that we haven't found time to unpack yet, we fall over it regularly in the kitchen. Most of my silver we have just put in a trunk as there is nowhere to keep it and certainly we won't be using it much while we are here. We didn't even get our coffee pot unpacked until last night.

Thursday and Friday of last week were days of domestic tragedies. The water system for some mysterious reason froze up completely, and we couldn't get a drop of water all day, and also it meant that I couldn't use the kitchen stove at all either. Luckily there was a community supper at Glenwood that night, and we went to that and both stuffed ourselves, eating enough to do us all the next day in case we couldn't get any fire on then either (it cost us fifty cents for as much as we could possibly eat, and then when we left they gave us a huge box of food to take home). Friday morning the pump had for again some mysterious reason thawed out and there was water. Our theme song here on the island should be that negro slave song, "Cool Water". For a day or two there I had a feeling of deep envy for every farmhouse we passed that had a "wee hoose" out back. Then on Friday we went to O'Leary and had our first car trouble—it was just dirt in the gas but it was enough to stop the car and hold us up for about three hours in the metropolis. We got back at about 6.15 and the people were coming in for a reception at 8.00 and we had been unpacking all morning and the place was a shambles. And inevitably one farmer came an hour early so that he could have a little chat with the minister before the company arrived. We also had YPU and Ladies Aid last week and last night Board of Stewards here at the manse. Tonight I have to go to a play practice down the road for a play the Ladies Aid is putting on. Tomorrow night YPU again. So far nothing for Thursday or Friday nights—we're keeping our fingers crossed. Saturday night I actually got some thank you letters written—Sunday nights we're too utterly tired, Blair from preaching three times, me from listening three times, to do anything but relax completely.

Presents are still coming in—this morning I got my third silver cake server, this one from people on the field. The outstanding present since I last wrote came from Saskatoon from Jean Quick. It is a little three-legged stool, beautifully made by herself, with a little note glued on the top "For Milking". Blair thinks it a very weird present, but I notice that he keeps it beside him in the kitchen all the time with his overflowing ash tray on it. From the Macleans in Sydney came a wonderful present, and one which we needed muchly—a carving set. It came yesterday, which was also the day that I cooked my first roast so it went into use immediately. Also beautiful hand made doilies from Joan Smith, a former maid of ours.

Blair got some new clothes in Summerside, an immense pair of fleece lined snow boots and the most tremendous fur hat, both of which he wears most of the time (outdoors, that is). I would like to have a snap of him in hat, boots, and itchy underwear, it would be a masterpiece! The weather stays amazingly mild, with the roads still open. Old timers say that they can never remember a winter like this. There was about eight inches of snow last week so he put chains on for Sunday but we really didn't need them.

This is all that I shall write this time. The church reports are nearly finished and so I must get dinner on the table so that we can set out for O'Leary. Here's hoping that the gas is clean.

As I look this letter over, I seem to have a long list of woes—It doesn't say anything about the tremendous enjoyment we are getting out of this new life together. Anyway, we are, even the woes are fun when we're in it together.

With lots of love,

Joan

Dear All of you,

For the first time it is looking like winter here on the Island. The snow really came on Friday night and on Saturday we woke to a white world. On Saturday afternoon just at sunset we went for a walk and it was simply beautiful. The wind came up though on Saturday night and snow drifted all night, and on Sunday we found to our sorrow that the beauty was only skin deep—or something, but more of that later.

Tonight is another evening at home—Praise the Lord. Tomorrow night the people of Cape Wolfe are holding a shower for us down there at the community hall. Blair says that such occasions are to be dreaded like anything and avoided if at all possible. We are therefore hoping for another storm, but chances for it seem slim.

Last week was quite uneventful, except that it went so Fast! My housekeeping is still something that I simply can't keep up with. I just get things clean and they are dirty again. I did my first laundry, and all the neighbors are going to be talking, because it didn't go out till two o'clock in the afternoon. And then followed my first struggles with those irons—Blair's white shirt I had to redampen three times before I was through, and then it didn't exactly look like a professional job. But I really am getting on to them now, and when I do my second laundry tomorrow morning I expect to just whip through it. The water system has been behaving admirably and we are just keeping our fingers crossed. One event of importance was our first attempts at using the cookie press! My husband finally persuaded me to try it (ever since I unpacked it and showed it to him he has been at me to use it)—so I mixed up the batter and he happily experimented with stars and hearts and curls, and now we have so many cookie press cookies that I don't ever want to see another again. And he is disappointed because I say that I will never use it again—unless <u>he</u> washed the hundred and one parts that go to make it up. We spent one evening headach-ing over a year's budget. At last inspection, we plan to spend $150 more than we will make this year. I think we need the finance minister, Mr. Abbott. But we are certainly eating cheaply and well because people are so very kind. On Friday morning a man brought in a beautiful T-bone roast, and after church last night another farmer handed me a huge sirloin roast. We cut the undercut from the latter and tonight for supper had the most out of this world filet mignon I ever hope to eat. And thick cream continues to flow in, and last week we also had about four pounds of wonderful salty dairy butter given to us.

Presents are still coming in, a pair of silver salts and peppers from Bobbie Allen, a quite unusual and rather atrocious pitcher from one of Blair's Pine Hill friends, and a beautiful bonbon dish of that frail Irish China from Edna Taylor of Sydney. And thank you letters still darken the light-heartedness of our days—there are still so many to write.

Sunday was Quite a Day. Our first service in the morning was right here in Springfield. It was a sunny looking winter day so we decided to walk the three-quarters of a mile or so to church. There was a bitter wind blowing, but it wasn't bad and anyway someone picked us up half-way there. Back for a rushed dinner and Blair put the chains on the car and we started for Cape Wolfe. We found when we got to the shore that the Strait was frozen as far out as we could see, the snow had drifted across the road a couple of feet deep in some places, and only a big truck had been there before us and its tracks were much deeper than ours, so there followed an exciting ride. We simply plunged into the drifts trying to keep in his ruts while the snow kept flying up against the windshield. And we did pretty well for a while but then got completely stuck in a snowbank and had to get dug out. To church on time and then started home again but this time we landed in the ditch and had to get dug out again, so we decided that for the evening we would go by horse and sleigh. The man next door took us out to Glenwood. The wind had gone down and the sky was full of stars—a perfect night for a sleigh ride, except that the same drifts meant that large sections of the road had no snow at all. It took us an hour to get the four miles or so through the woods to that point. As the farmer who took us laconically remarked— "It would be a pretty slow way to start going around the world". It is just a little sleigh, with room for two to sit, so I had to sit on my husband's knee and on the way back my big roast of beef sat on mine. Were we ever glad to get back to our own nice comfortable kitchen! At that point my husband ordered bacon and eggs, and we relaxed, listening to the Four Gentlemen and Stage 49.

And now another week has started. Poor Blair had to spend the afternoon with Mrs. Frizzle, while I spent a much more pleasant p.m. washing floors and socks and making cookies (without the cookie press).

And that seems to be the news to date—nothing earthshaking, just common day to day living, but it's kind of fun.

Love to all of you,

Joan

```
               O'Leary r.r. I
                  Spud Island
                    Jan. 31st.
```

Hello there—

January 31st! We wish to report the accomplishment of one month
of married life with no casualties other than a couple of pairs of rather
more calloused hands than previously, one pair of housemaid's knees, a
couple of plates, and a sparkplug or two (from the car). I'm ashamed to
admit that yesterday both of us had forgotten that we had reached such
an important anniversary—but not so our congregations: at three different points yesterday we were greeted by someone saying in sympathetic
tones, "Well, the honeymoon is over". And so a month that has been a
lot of fun and a lot of work, which has brought strange new changes to
both of us is over, and it has been a very rich and a very good month.

We have just returned from visiting, our first expedition of this sort.
We left here at 1.15 p.m, and got back at a quarter to nine. Apparently
visiting has a habit of turning out that way round here. Of the five places
we visited, three asked us to stay for supper—at the last place we stayed.
Everywhere they seemed awfully glad of a visit from the preacher—but
it depressed me, for every home had such a spotlessly clean kitchen
floor, and I kept remembering how very much ours needed scrubbing.
Now we are back in our own dirty floored kitchen waiting for a certain
program to come on our radio, Dorothy Sayers' twelve radio plays on
the life of Christ, "The Man Born to be King", are being presented each
Monday night from now to Easter over CBC. Listen some night, because
her plays are by far the best things of that sort I have ever heard.

You remember that I said in my last letter that the congregation of
Cape Wolfe were planning a reception for us last Tuesday night. The
arrangement was that we were to go if the weather was good. That is
an awkward arrangement to make at any time, especially as the last
wind blew all the telephone lines between here and there down. Tuesday dawned bright and sunny but with a fast descending temperature
and a rising wind with subsequent drifting snow. By 7.00 it was zero
and the wind was blowing like sixty, or at least like twenty-five. We

wouldn't have started at all except that we knew that the snow plow had been down there in the morning, and we knew that they knew that we knew—therefore we were pretty sure they would expect us. And so we started off. I had a premonition that we would never make it, so just before we left I pulled my old slacks over my dress. We got a mile and a half and the car just simply stopped and refused to go any farther. We hadn't even run thru any big drifts, it was sheer insubordination on the part of the car. So we simply left the car there for the night and walked home. We found we had a great many things for which to be thankful, 1) the wind was behind us, 2) We didn't have to go to the reception, 3) we hadn't got any farther, and 4) I had my slacks on. The walk home was not exactly pleasant but Blair pulled town the ear lugs on his fur hat, and my coon coat would keep out the severest blast. So we came home and lit a fire in the kitchen stove and spent a warm and pleasant evening at home.

That seems to have been our one adventure for the week. Otherwise we are continuing to become very domesticated people as we do our fire-watching, cooking, etc. I made a pie this week—butterscotch, and it really wasn't too awful. By doing three laundries this week and by washing four pairs of socks every day and a half (we have only four sock stretchers!) I am slowly coming to the end of the immense pile of dirty clothes which my husband managed to collect during his batching days. The laundry business here has been revolutionized here by the discovery of the bathtub. The water goes into it and out of it without the assistance of hundreds of buckets, and while it means that I wash humbly on my knees—it's worth it.

More wedding presents this week. We went into O'Leary on Tuesday afternoon and picked up four express parcels—a wooden tray from John Hibbitts, a Dal friend of us both—three beautiful cups and saucer from Mr. and Mrs. J. L. Ilsley—a silver tea stand from Mr. and Mrs. Guy of Saint John—a pair of silver candle sticks from Judge Graham of Halifax. Then on Friday we received three beautiful crotcheted pieces (pineapple pattern) from Mr. and Mrs. Clifford Archibald of Truro.

Yesterday was the last Sunday in January, and we got to all the points by car—and all the roads were good. It was a bitterly cold day, and Blair wore his immense fleece-lined boots with his black suit and clerical collar for preaching. But it really is amazing to have the roads open here at this time of year. We were invited out for dinner after church, and we have discovered a very interesting point about West Cape etiquette "when entertaining the minister"—and it is in relation to serviettes. On Sunday Nine people had dinner at the table, but in setting it seven paper serviettes and two linen ones were put on—the two latter for the preacher and his wife. And this evening at supper there were only two serviettes on the table—for us not for anyone else.

I here quote a choice item from the Charlottetown Guardian, it being a telling comment on both Island morals and Journalism. The interesting part of it, aside from its intrinsic merit is the fact that it was sent to the paper by the Rev. Mr. Dickson himself: "On Sunday afternoon, Jan. 23rd at the home of the grandparents, Mr. and Mrs. John Williams in O'Leary, Rev. W. G. Dickson baptized the infant son of Mr. and Mrs. George Austin Hays, Gregory George, who was born in Summerside on Feb. 23rd, 1948. Mr. and Mrs. Hays were the first couple married by Rev. Mr. Dickson when he came to the O'Leary Pastoral Charge in August of 1947, their marriage taking place on August 18th, 1947."

Seems like that's all for now, folks.

So long for now,

From the Manse in what
promises to be a
BLIZZARD
February 8th

Dear Folks,

   With the wind howling about the house and the snow blowing against the windows, here by the light of the oil lamp two people sit disconsolately in this Garden of the Gulf. We are disconsolate for two reasons: 1) after being snow bound for six days Blair finally after hours of hard labour shovelled out our driveway today so that we could get the car out—and right now it's drifting in again far faster than he shovelled out. That's depressing. 2) Tomorrow Presbytery meets in Charlottetown, and the Colbornes planned to drive over for it, the weatherman willing (he isn't going to be). No trip to New York or Bagdad was ever more eagerly discussed, planned for or awaited than that one to the Metropolis. But it seems to be all off and we feel very sorry for ourselves. Luckily we got into O'Leary this afternoon while it was still fine (the first time in two weeks) and got our shopping done and letters mailed and a haircut for the man of the family and a visit paid to Mr. and Mrs. Dickson. So the shovelling was not completely in vain!

   You must have wondered why our last letter took such a long time between writing and arriving. The answer is of course—the Weather. For winter really set in in earnest here last Tuesday, lots of snow and below zero temperatures and high winds. Some days the mailman didn't get through at all, and each night our mailbox got chock full of snow. Getting through to the store just four farms from us was in itself quite an expedition, it involved getting into ski pants and wading through three foot drifts. Then the snow drifted and hardened leaving all over the place drifts sometimes over five feet high so hard that a horse and sleigh could go right over top of them. Thursday was the most bitterly cold and windy day of them all, so it was of course the day that Blair had a funeral way down the shore road about five miles. The man next door took him in an open sleigh and boy was he cold when it was all over—it must have been ten below with a 45 mile wind. They tell us that people down the shore road always pick this time of year to die.

35 Joan Archibald Colborne

Because we were in all week, news is very scarce. Mail is the big event each day and we eagerly await it. And how wonderful you have all been about writing to us. We've heard from the three Colbornes and three Archibalds since the last time we wrote, and other relatives and friends have been very good about writing to us. My former room-mates in Sarnia sent me a cheque this week for my share of the furniture in our apartment and I'm going to spend it on furniture for the manse. Positively the first thing we're going to get is a rocking chair for the kitchen. We have one in it now, but the difficulty is that we're always both wanting to sit in it at the same times (which is of course very nice once in a while, but we can't do it all the time). Then we'll get a little gas cooking stove with one burner for use in the summer when it's very hot (that seems a long way off tonight). And wedding presents continue to come in, we've had two this week. The Plants of Moncton sent us a beautiful round mirror. We're going to put it over the mantle in the livingroom, where it will be a great blessing, as pictures get rather lost in the midst of such loud and boisterous wall paper.

Blair favours hanging it in the bathroom so that he won't have to shave at the kitchen sink, and that would be nice, but it doesn't seem to me that it's exactly a bathroom mirror, and we can probably get a five and ten cent store one for that purpose. Then the Gerald Martins sent us a dear little knocker for the front door. It is brass and really very cute. There has been some discussion over that present too. I thought that the figure on it was the Devil and therefore a rather funny present to send to a manse—but Blair said it was a pixie—close inspection of the knocker revealed that it said it was a pixie, but it still looks like the devil to me. My thank you letters this week have been reduced from twenty six to fourteen which is certainly a help, and a couple more weeks of being snowbound should see the end of them.

Yesterday was rather a peculiar Sunday because I only went to church once instead of three times. Roads were still blocked so he had to go to Cape Wolfe and Glenwood by sleigh, and as sleighs were constructed for pairs and not trios I was really quite content to let Blair and the driver be the pair. Mr. Collicut our next door neighbor drove him. I give thanks daily that we didn't undertake to keep a horse. It would be such a headache. Yesterday was a beautiful day, cold but calm. In the evening we had church here so we walked to the church—I don't know when I've been out on a more perfect evening. And we got a sleigh ride home in which we dashed through the snow just exactly the way you're supposed to in a sleigh. It was queer having my husband away all day. One minister's wife I was talking to before I got married, said the only thing wrong with marrying a minister was that "they're under foot all the time". And it is true—there are times when I'm baking or getting the kitchen floor scrubbed, that I think it would be wonderful to have a husband you just ship off to the office every morning and welcome home at night. But you know with these guys who are underfoot all the time, you sure miss them when they're not around.

I have just asked my husband if there is any more news that I should pass on to you. He informs me that I have not mentioned the fact that he froze the middle finger of his right hand at the funeral on Thursday. Don't worry about it, it seems to have thawed since—and for some unaccountable reason he seems proud of it.

Our love to you all,

O'Leary R.R. #1
P. E. I.
February 16th

Dear People,

    As I look at the calendar I see that it is quite a time since you heard from this part of the country. February is certainly flying by. It's amazing how quickly the time goes even though our activities outside of the house have been limited to going for the milk and down to the mail box (Sunday excepted) since we last wrote. And now this will be just a note to let you know that we are alive still because really there is no news.

    We have been pretty well housed because of snow. It meant missing two WMS meetings and one Ladies Aid meeting and one Young Peoples meeting last week—and we won't get to YPU again tonight. We were not heart broken. It's not that it is very bad winter weather, just very frequent—as soon as the roads are open from one snow fall another occurs. It snowed last night, but today is very mild, in fact the house got so hot that we had to have the front door open most of this afternoon! The nights are simply beautiful now, it is just about full moon and the countryside is covered with snow and really it is just about as light as day. Why in the evening after supper, it is almost a pleasure to go out and empty the slop pail (I know that my husband will remark when he reads this, "Well, why don't you do it more often?") There are certain aspects of this rural life that I feel sorry for you city people having to miss.

    February 14th was Valentine's Day—and say, you were so good about remembering us! We appreciated Ed's lovely card, and certainly the box of chocolates from Sydney brought a great deal of pleasure, and with that cheque from Ottawa we have ordered a new battery for the radio. Our radio is getting very dim, and I no longer listen with one very vague ear to the soap operas as I work—we are rationing our listening until the village store gets the battery. The news, the weather forecast, Musically Yours with Elwood Glover and our old pal Rawhide are the only things we listen to. And by the way, do you people listen to Rawhide? As Blair says, it's the "loveliest" program. Comes on at 9.30 a.m. Atlantic and 8.30 Eastern Standard time. If you don't abhor it you'll adore it. We adore it. We celebrated Valentine's Day by making a journey to the local store which is always quite an occasion—while I shop Blair talks—and we bought among other things a rat trap, the most wicked looking contraption. We brought it home and set it and caught one within fifteen minutes. Our score of rodents since arrival is now four mice and two rats. Just wait until spring comes and the skunks wake up! Or are they rodents, and how do you catch them anyway?

One fascinating part of our life here is our telephone, for the first month our ring never rang, but we have had three or four calls in the last week—and when we finally realize that that is our number which is being called there is wild excitement, and whichever one of us has a throat in the best condition rushes to the phone and simply bellows "Hello!!!" Then you hear something faintly at the other end saying "I can't hear you" to which you shriek, "I can't hear you either!!!" This goes on until Central intervenes and says in exasperation, "Will all you people put your receivers down". And then lo, presto—you can almost hear who is trying to get you and what they want. Apparently there is not always this difficulty, tho it is never easy—but when the manse number rings every receiver in the community comes off the hook.

Believe it or not there are still wedding presents coming in. We got a sterling butter knife in our silver set from Mary MacKeigan and a beautiful sterling butter dish with a knife also in our pattern from Judge and Mrs. Carroll of Halifax, a little silver bon-bon dish from the Buchanans of Sydney, and a tea pot from Mr. and Mrs. Percy Cuthbert of Halifax. We now have six tea pots, and three of them are three sizes of the same pattern, white with gold wiggles.

Yesterday in an excess of zeal I managed to get my husband working hanging our mirrors and pictures, putting up the full length one was quite a job for it is very heavy, but after I had stood holding it for hours and hours and hours while he measured and moved it, he made an excellent job of putting it up. Now I can see if my slip is showing before he informs me of it.

Sunday is always such an exciting day in our uneventful week. It is filled with the element of the unexpected as we are never quite sure whether or not we will get to the point we set out for or not, and Say, last Sunday really lived up to all our expectations and unexpectations. First service was here in Springfield, good crowd out, the car was on its best behavior over the whole mile and a half there and back. Next was Cape Wolfe and they had plowed the road so it was a really easy jaunt. Cape Wolfe is fortunate in having an active CCF element in the population, and the government keeps the roads out that way well plowed in an effort to win some of the wanderers back into the fold—election coming up. But unfortunately Glenwood is a solid old liberal district, no danger of Glenwood moving left or right. Therefore the snowplow is seldom round there, so Glenwood is usually our big problem on Sundays. By horse and sleigh it is just about three and a half miles through the fields. But it was a very wettish snowy night and if we could possibly get there by car we didn't want to go by sleigh. We heard that if we went in to O'Leary and took a road out from there we would get there all right because they'd been hauling fertilizer out that way on Saturday. So we set out by car. And it was a good road—for about the first fifteen miles. Then it didn't seem to be very plowed any more and about three miles from the church the car jumped out of the rut and landed in the deep snow and refused to budge. It was half an hour to church time and we were right in front of the home of one of the Catholic families in the district, so we went in for help. While I visited with the wife the men tried to get the car unstuck, but even the tractor wouldn't work it out and it was getting nearer and nearer church time. So then the man got out the sleigh and said he would take us to church. Just as we were about to leave he suggested that Blair take the sleigh himself and bring it back after church. He said, "The mare is good, only she is a little wicked. She is fine, except that she is hard to stop". Blair hesitated like he might say yes, so I felt that I had kept a wifely silence long enough and I spoke up and insisted that he come along with us. Anyway we had a good swift sleigh ride to church and got there only about five minutes late. During churchtime the man got a truck, got the car unstuck and drove it in to Glenwood and it was waiting for us when we were finished. Now wasn't that good of him—and he was a Catholic too. Like the wisemen we went back another way, which if we had really been wise we would have started out in the first place. All in all we went forty miles in our trip to and from church that night—as far as from here to Summerside, so it was Quite A Night.

When I started this letter this afternoon I decided that there wasn't enough to write about to cover one page, but I seem to have talked on and on about nothing. Since I started it Blair has completed shovelling out the driveway for the umpteenth time, we have had supper, washed up and now the lamps are lit and we are settled down for a nice quiet evening at home—for a change! Rats and snow drifts and slop pails and so many quiet evenings at home—it's a funny thing, but as my husband said the other day, "There's something that somehow seems to make up for it all".

Love from us to all of you,

```
                              The Manse
                                O' Leary R. R. #1
                                P. E. I.
```

February 25th

Hello Folks,

Well, what do you know—February is just about over! I think it was so nice of the Lord, or whoever did it, to put the shortest month of the year just where it is, because it is just where psychologically we need a good short month. It would be so sad if June or July or August or September had only twenty-eight days. At least March <u>sounds</u> as if the winter was nearly over. The way it is snowing here tonight I have the feeling that winter is still very much with us—but it is almost March!

My husband has been very busy since I last wrote—with funerals. In the last nine days he has had three. This afternoon he went by horse and sleigh to bury an old lady, then last week he buried two babies, one was born about three weeks ago and the other was a most pathetic funeral on a cold windy day down at the shore. Now whenever the phone rings or anyone comes to the door we're scared that it may be another funeral.

Our radio battery came on Saturday, much to our relief. We certainly depend on that radio for entertainment. Last Friday night it had got so desperately weak that if we chewed we couldn't hear it—and whenever the point of a joke came one of us would move, or a coal would fall in the fire, or some other great noise would intervene and we would miss it. What is more maddening? So we decided that it was just too hard on our nerves and we would simply not use it till the battery came. And to our amazement, on Saturday morning we went over to the store and there it was. So we now have a schedule of all our pet programs for the week pinned on our bulletin board so we won't miss any. Tonight Blair gets his mental stimulation for the week with Beat the Champs (that's the way he describes it—I consider it rather rude when he has such a mentally stimulating wife to talk to and argue with.) Tomorrow I keep up with the current songs with the Hit Parade. I wonder what people in the country did before they had radios.

Sunday as usual was the event of the week for adventures. Glenwood in the morning, and we took the car and went the twenty miles under the erroneous impression (gained thru much bellowing at the phone Saturday night) that it was plowed all the way to the church. We got to within three miles and the plowed road simply stopped, and then what a three miles! However we didn't get stuck until we were within a mile of the church and then only twice and there were some good church members near to dig us out. We were invited out to dinner at Glenwood and then our hosts followed us out the three miles to give assistance in case of difficulty and after that it was clear sailing. But it had started to snow and drift so it didn't look too good for Cape Wolfe, our evening service. One of the men in the Springfield congregation offered to take us in the evening, by horse if it looked too bad, otherwise in his car. He was an optimist and arrived with the car, well stocked with shovels and two other men. I was a little fed up with being stuck in snow drifts so I declined to attend church that evening—thank heaven! It is five miles to Cape Wolfe, it took them an hour to make it going down. It took them well over two hours and a half to get back—and they had a team of horses pulling the car most of the way and four men shovelling and pushing. It was twenty after eleven when Blair returned home, looking just like a snowman.

Monday was a most beautiful, sunny, snowy day after the storm— and of course Monday is parson's day off. He spent a large part of it shovelling (good for his waistline), and we went for a walk, and also took a roll of film—yes, those long-awaited pictures at last. We're sending them to Charlottetown to have them developed, and will send them as soon as we get them back. Then we made a momentous decision—it being our day off, we would go into O'Leary—and go to the MOVIES, provided the picture was not utterly hopeless or we hadn't seen it too many times before—we weren't really fussy. We got combed and shaved and dressed and then in high excitement and expectation started off. And here comes the Tragedy of the week. There was no movie in O'Leary that night. Due to the burning of the power plant there last week electricity was rationed and movies were only shown on Fridays and Saturdays. Isn't that a sad story?

But we did get our entertainment this week—and from a source we had never thought would be really entertaining. The Ladies Aid of the Springfield church put on two one act plays and a sort of variety concert last night. Blair was asked to be master of ceremonies and we went with sort of a "Duty Bound" attitude. We certainly weren't looking forward to it. It was a lovely clear cold starlight night and we walked to the community hall. It was a little stuffy building—the stage was about as big as a postage stamp and some of the players didn't know their parts. But <u>did we ever</u> enjoy it! Every song, every reading, every funny bit in the plays we just lapped up. They sold bags of home made fudge at intermission and I found myself sitting right on the edge of my chair, sucking fudge, my eyes and ears just glued on that little postage stamp of a stage. It wasn't only that the Colbornes were kind of starved for entertainment, there was some good stuff there—a couple of the men were excellent actors and carried the plays, and a couple of very talented kids put over their cowboy music in the most outgoing enthusiastic way. Any way it was a big success.

I'm going to stop now for it is time for my husband to have his mental stimulation for the week, and I must not type through that!

So, bye for now, and more anon......

With our love,

Being an epistle written to those who live in
Civilization from the Pioneers on this day of
grace March the Third in the year of our Lord
nineteen hundred and forty nine.

Greetings:

At the outset I would like to ask each of you to consign to the fire the last
letter which you received from us, for in it I made certain foolish and
optimistic remarks about the grand spring like feeling that it gave one to
feel that March was so near. Springlike. That's actually what I said. And
here we are completely snowbound with drifts four and five feet high
surrounding the house. Even the people who have lived round here all
their life have been impressed with this series of blizzards.

It started on Saturday afternoon (the snowplow came out here Saturday morning, first time in a week, and opened the road between here
and O'Leary). It was snowing and blowing pretty hard when we went
out to the store about three o'clock to send a telegram, and by four the
roads were impassable again. The wind and the snow roared around the
house all night. We awoke Sunday morning to brilliant sunshine—and
a fifty mile an hour wind. The snow was drifting so hard and fast that in
spite of an absolutely clear blue sky we couldn't see the house across
the street all day. Drifts of from four to eight feet lay across the road just
in the quarter mile between the manse and the store. Blair had made arrangements with one of the men near by to be driven by sleigh to Cape
Wolfe in the morning and Glenwood in the afternoon. We hoped the
man wouldn't be crazy enough to venture out. He wasn't. So we spent a
delightful Sunday at home, just sitting and reading. By evening the wind
had died down, so we decided that we had better show up at church. It
was to be a joint service in the Springfield Baptist Church. So we walked
to the church—and it was quite an expedition! The snow had drifted so
hard that we walked on top of it all the way up and down the drifts—and
for most of our journey we were the only people who had set foot on it
all day—not a person or horse and sleigh had been over it before us. Six
people were at church, and none of them included anyone who could
play the organ so we had a very informal service without any singing.
Then the long trek (must be all of half a mile, but it took us half an hour
to do it) home. Monday dawned fine—no mailman came but a num-

ber of sleighs broke a sort of a road. Tuesday was a great day—the Mail finally came, but on Tuesday night it started storming again and from then until Wednesday night it stormed. It was terrific. When one of us went out to the end of the house to empty the slop pail on Wednesday we would come in looking like a member of an Antarctic expedition, simply covered with snow. I was getting sick of indoors by afternoon so I volunteered to go over to the house across the road for the milk—and to get across the road I had to wade through snow up to my hips. I nearly gave up, but finally won through. Today was beautiful, but impossible walking, most difficult sleighing, and as for cars, why we've practically forgotten what one looks like. And this morning when I was talking to the farmer next door he said, That sky looks like we're in for more snow! People feel that it will be a long time before the snow plow opens this road again, and when it finally does we still have a good four-foot drift reaching from the garage right down to the road, and all of it across the driveway.

Our friend the mailman came today and ironically enough he brought a letter from a couple whom we know, Kay and Al Finlay. Their big news was that Al's doctor had informed him that he was tired out and needed rest and sun, so they are starting out this week for the West Indies. As soon as Blair heard that he decided to walk into O'Leary and see the doctor—by the end of that walk he would be worn out enough to have rest and sun recommended. All day at intervals one or other of us can be heard muttering, "the West Indies".

There are other difficulties involved in this business of being snowed in. For one thing, we have been getting our meat supply from O'Leary and a diet of bacon and eggs and Kam is beginning to pall. And another thing my husband gets in town is haircuts, and he is beginning to have a rather artistic appearance.

But the real tragedy was the fact that Mum couldn't get over to the Island for this coming weekend. She wired on Saturday that she could come and were we ever excited! It would have been such a break in the winter. So many things we wanted to tell her and show her, and any weekend in January or February would have been fine. But not this week. We were frightfully disappointed.

Yesterday in the middle of the storm we looked out our diningroom window to see <u>eight</u> <u>partridge</u> sheltering in the lee of the house. We longed for a gun in our meatless state.

This is not a very interesting letter—seems to be rather one track, but our life has been of necessity forced into that one track, and unless you would like a brief review of all the books we have gobbled up in the last few days, this is all there is to say.

Except that in spite of all we decided by mutual consent today—we still think that it is awfully nice being married to each other.

with our love,

```
            The Manse,
               O'Leary R.R.  1,  PEI
                  March 10th
```

Dear People,

Here once again is your weekly report of the life and adventures of that fascinating young couple, the Colbornes, and their battle with the elements, and the rodents, and once in a while, the congregation.

First of all the weather report: For four days in a row now we have had freezing rain and everything in sight is covered with ice. Walking is almost impossible, it is just one long slide from our front door to the gate. The snow plow finally came out on Tuesday for the first time in ten days and all the men in the community got out with shovels and dug it out of frozen snowbank after frozen snowbank. The frustrating part of it was that even though Blair shovelled hard with them, the plow stopped a hundred yards from our gate and went back home and we haven't seen it since, nor do we expect to until spring.

I have been to two meetings this week, so the social element in this life is really flourishing. On Friday afternoon the United Church and Baptist women came together for the World Day of Prayer meeting. It was a very small gathering as the roads were impassable, but such a meeting is always rather a thrilling thing as the realization comes that all over the world on that day women are meeting together to pray. The Baptist ladies were hostesses and they served tea and <u>quantities</u> of food after the prayer meeting. The amount of food that people eat here on the island is simply prodigious. Do you know that the Ladies Aid here decided that too much food was being served so they limited the amount to <u>five</u> different kinds of food, and the person at whose home the meeting is being held has to provide it all. I am hesitating to invite the group to the manse until I learn to make five different kinds of things fairly well and certainly. Then the Springfield West Women's Institute met on Tuesday night, of which group I am now a member. They have not limited the food there yet, we had seven different kinds.

Sunday was a day of great tragedy—though it was kind of a funny tragedy! We had church here in the morning and in the afternoon one of the neighbors took Blair to Cape Wolfe and it was on the way there that the accident occurred. Sleighing is quite a business with the great peaks and hollows that the drifting snow makes across the roads, and every now and then the sleigh goes down into what is called a pitch which is just a particularly deep hollow. On the road to Cape Wolfe the sleigh hit a pitch, such a one that the horse came loose and left the sleigh and the two men sitting in the hollow, and in the jolt Blair managed to sit on a nail and tear a large triangular rip in the seat of his brown suit. And then he had to go into the pulpit with the rip in full view of the congregation on the way up. I laughed and laughed when he came home, but it really wasn't very funny, as aside from his black suit that is all he has, and a tailor is something unknown around these parts. With a great effort we managed to get him into an old blue suit for the evening service at Glenwood, and aside from the fact that he found breathing difficult and certainly couldn't let himself go with any great emotional force during the sermon, it was all right. But what we do now we are not very sure.

As radio forms such a large and important part of our life and that man Rawhide is our radio highlight every day we were of course very interested and concerned about all the stir caused by his program. If the CBC tries to take him away from us we will write long and violent letters to the government and the Board of Governors and all the newspapers we can think of.

I had prided myself on having acquired such an even-tempered husband—now at last I have found the two words that never fail to get his temper up and make him a difficult man to live with. Those two words are these: George Drew. And unfortunately the two newspapers we get every day are the Post Record and the Guardian both of which every day have at least one, usually two editorials on the brilliance, the exploits, the force of Gorgeous George, so each morning there are a couple of explosions followed by suppressed mutterings that go on all day. And may I say that on this subject I am a very sympathetic listener.

And now we would like to tell you about a little addition to the Colborne family. Surprised? Well don't get any ideas, this was a dog. And to tell you the story you must first understand two things, us and dogs, and Mrs. Frizzle. We have been having an argument about dogs for quite a while—I would like to have a dog, my husband says no, except if we can get a really good dog, not one of the mongrels they grow round here, but preferably no dog, we have nothing to feed dogs and they make puddles, etc. Now Mrs. Frizzle I have mentioned before. Her dog had nine puppies and she has been trying to get rid of them, on us in particular, and we were most unenthusiastic. On Tuesday night we were having a very late and rushed supper when a knock came at the door and there was a boy who handed me a dog and said here's your dog and disappeared. Blair recognized him as a Frizzle and was raging, but we seemed to be stuck with a dog, and I was rather pleased. It was a sort of cute little pup, reportedly part collie. But then I took a closer look and I was raging—it was a female dog. So I said, We're not keeping this dog. Meanwhile the dog made her first puddle. I was due at Women's Institute, and as there was a chance of Letty (Mrs. Frizzle) being there we decided that dog or no dog I had better go and leave this new addition with my husband, who could never be termed a dog lover. Meanwhile the dog made another puddle. My husband was muttering something about "the bitch" under his breath, and I guess he meant the dog. As I went out the door he was preparing to wipe up another puddle, and he yelled after me, "If we keep her, we call her Letty". We had found a big packing box in which we had put Letty and as I passed our rose bush on the way out I heard her barking and whining in loud and piteous tones. It was a long meeting, and it was three and a half hours later that I passed the rose bush again only to hear exactly the same whining and barking. She had never let up the whole time. Blair had been planning to work on his sermon that evening. Ha. Ha. Was he ever a frazzled, orFrizzled, character when I arrived back! Next morning we wrapped Letty in a blanket and put her in a shopping bag and Blair set out with great annoyance and much muttering to return her. We've decided not to get a dog.

The last straw of Tuesday came as I went past the barn that night—a faint <u>but unmistakable</u> whiff of skunk. Our first sign that spring is nearly here.

Will spring really come? Will Blair's trousers be able to be repaired? Will George Drew be the next Prime Minister? Will the Colbornes get rid of the skunks? or will the skunks get rid of the Colbornes? Will there be another addition to the Colborne family? Tune in again next week for another exciting installment of "Life Can Be Beautiful".

This is station P.E.I. signing off for the evening,

With love,

Joan

Hello Folks,

Our calendar tells us that it is today the day before the first day of Spring. It's funny but the weather man here on the Island doesn't seem to have realized it yet. It blew and drifted all night and today the man who was to have taken Blair to Cape Wolfe this morning decided that even his horse couldn't get through those roads. They're trying to get to Glenwood this afternoon, but whether they will make it or not is still a question. And we have a new drift at least seven feet high in front of the garage door. So it isn't exactly springlike yet!

This letter is late this week, but it's been a very busy week, and I have decided to change our letter writing day to Sunday until I can get around the field with my husband again. It makes a terribly long day with so little to do.

Last Sunday it started to melt underneath the snow, and what a mess. Blair got around to all points, but I guess it was a very difficult trip and on the morning trip to Glenwood they tried to go through the woods and nearly got dumped into a swamp which had become unfrozen. I wasn't so fortunate—I didn't get to church at all. We started out though to walk to Bethel, and all was fine until we just about got to the church when I fell into a puddle under the snow and just filled my snow boots with icy water, so I turned around and trudged home. No cold or ill effect of any sort followed, except that Blair informed me that I missed his best sermon of the last three months.

Blair has been going so hard this week, that if he doesn't lose a few pounds this week he never will. On Monday, a beautiful day, he set out to pay a sick call which was quite a walk—eight miles, round trip. Another funeral on Tuesday. A snowstorm on Wednesday, as a result of which he shovelled snow all day Thursday. Sermon writing Friday, and then wonder of wonders—he got a sleigh ride to O'Leary yesterday.

That trip to O'Leary was a long-awaited thing. It is over a month since we have been there. He was to have gone with the man across the road on Thursday, going in with a load of feed and coming back with a load of fertilizer. But the storm intervened. However on Saturday morning one or the chaps down the road called to say that he was leaving for town with a load of potatoes in twenty minutes and he would take him if he could be ready. Well, could he ever be! So he went to town and got some Meat, and a Haircut, and some Money, and ordered some Coal, and brought me back two Magazines. It was wonderful. And last night we had pork chops for dinner, and today we had hamburgers, and tomorrow we're going to cook a roast. What utter bliss.

I've had three meetings this week, one of the Ladies Aid and two committee meetings of the Women's Institute. The Women's Institute is having a Social "Time" in the community hall on Tuesday night and I am in charge of the program committee to provide games for the evening. Two very bright young girls from down the road are on it and they came up to the manse on Tuesday night to plan the program. I provided food for them, but they had to leave early to go to a party and I thought, "What will I do with all this food". I needn't have worried. Blair had an official board meeting at the church, only the janitor had forgotten to put a fire on in the church, so he came back here with seven members. So we fed them. All in all it has been quite a week for visitors. On Wednesday evening a couple who go together here in the village came in and stayed for the evening. He is in the merchant marine on the Lake boats all summer and she is a clerk in the store. And we had to feed them— but we'd used all our food the night before! Then I remembered our wedding cake, stored away for such emergencies. Boy I was certainly glad we had it.

Last week was a grim week in one way—the mailman missed two days in a row, Wednesday and Thursday, no mail. But Friday was wonderful for we got three days' mail at once. Again we say how much your mail means to us. Oh yes and here I would like to put forward a plea. The Red Cross and Mount Allison and numerous other institutions are putting forth pleas at this time—the Colborne plea is for more onion skin letter paper like this. We got this in Summerside and are using our last sheet tonight—and Summerside seems very, very far away. So if you have enjoyed these letters and would like to see them continue, a few hundred sheets of paper would be greatly appreciated. I thank you.

<u>Sunday Evening</u>: In the middle of writing this letter I indulged in my usual Sunday afternoon activity—went fast asleep, and during that time a most unexpected thing happened—the snow plow came out almost to our gate. So now we hope we will be able to have our coal delivered on Monday. If we don't we'll be in a bad and cold way, for our supply is getting very low.

Blair got to and from Glenwood quite safely this afternoon and this evening we went to church. I had been over for the milk and the walking was so impossible that I decided that if we walked I simply would not go. However some people down the road called for us in a big wood sleigh. It was a beautiful evening, though frosty, but the roads were so terrible that we didn't think there would be anyone in church. But there were about ten sleighfulls there. It's fun afterward to see all the sleighs lined up and then going off in different directions into the night with sleigh bells ringing. The sleigh ahead of us tonight upset and the horse went rushing off home leaving its passengers to be picked up by the sleigh behind. That's the first upset we've seen. Wild excitement.

Well, I guess that's all for now—so bye for now,

With our love,

```
                              The Manse,
                           O'Leary RR 1
                                P.E.I.
                             March 27th
```

Dear Everybody,

Sunday afternoon again, and I have time to just get this letter started. While Blair is at service and a funeral I am going to visit with one of
the women in the congregation and then he will come to this home for
supper. A meal out is a great treat—one that I never fully appreciated
until I started preparing three meals a day.

A great thing happened this week—SPRING put in its first shy appearance! Ever since Wednesday the snow has been disappearing un-
believably quickly. Some of the fields are almost completely bare, and
the red mud is everywhere, I have never in my life before rejoiced to see
mud. There is still lots of snow on the banks but people are using their
cars again on the road to O'Leary—though the water is well over a foot
high in some places 'tis said. It's very messy dirty weather, but it's spring.
Last evening right after supper we went for a walk, all done up in rubber
boots, and we found ourselves acting just like kids again, clearing out
gutters for the water to flow down, pushing the slush away to make rivers and streams and waterfalls. Probably the congregation thought we
were a little nuts.

Tuesday was a great day for us—we had six letters, one from every
one of our mothers, fathers, brothers, sisters (well, the last two in the
singular).

Tuesday was also the Women's Institute social evening, to which I
had looked forward with a great deal of dread as I was in charge of the
program. We held it in the community hall, a terrible ramshackle old
place, and it was a strange meeting. There were about fifty there rang-
ing in age from six to well over sixty and we played games and ate and
then had a Share The Wealth program. One game in which you might be
interested was Forfeits. Apparently it is a standby round here. In order
to redeem his forfeit the United Church minister in these here parts had
to kiss the pretty girl who clerks in the store. He did it with great enthu-

siasm. On the whole I think the evening was a fair success though not a howling.

The funeral today is Blair's second for this week. There have certainly been an awful lot of them since we arrived.

We are hoping to get over to Halifax for Pine Hill Convocation on April 20th. Dad has offered us the trip over, and if we can drive at that time we will certainly go. The road between here and O'Leary will be the main difficulty, it may be an impossible, impassible sea of mud by that time. But wouldn't it be wonderful to get to Halifax again! It's over a month and a half now since I have been out of this community even to go to church and the thought of it—gosh. However in just about a month we're expecting a visit from the Colbornes, then in May one from the Archibalds, in June Conference at Sackville, in July Vacation School will keep us busy and August—holidays. So whether we get to Halifax or not, our long spell is about over. And we have really lived through it remarkably well. We suddenly realized last night that after three solid months of each other's company twenty-four hours a day and almost no relief in the form of other people to talk to—neither of us had been one bit bored! Of course we're both very interesting people!

As you can see, we got some more paper so these letters can continue—and for the rest of our lives judging by the amount of paper that arrived from Ottawa yesterday. I know that you will all be greatly relieved.

The skunks are getting worse—much worse. Every now and again we wake up at night and have to rush to the window and close it as the aroma is wafting into the bedroom. The best reason I have been able to find for keeping a horse is that it would have convinced the skunks that the barn was occupied.

Our coal came from O'Leary on Tuesday and we are now using it in the kitchen stove—and how I hate it after the nice clean wood. Everything is filthy all the time. And I don't think it's as good for cooking as wood—yesterday I baked a sponge cake and it went directly out of the oven into the fire. Blair says that I shouldn't blame it all on the coal, after all one needs to look at a fire occasionally during the cooking, or else why wouldn't it get low? Maybe sometime I'll remember that I'm not cooking with electricity—or gas!

Do you know that the wedding presents are still coming in! In the last couple of weeks we have received two pairs of silver salts and peppers, one from the Currahs of Bright, Ont., and one from Dorothy and Charlie Fowler of Halifax. Also a weird thing for serving pies in, silver from Mr. and Mrs. Tom Read of Ottawa.

Monday Evening: No mail today and so no chance to get this mailed so I'll add a note to it. We had hoped to get to O'Leary this week but the roads are bad—we went for a walk this evening and at one place the water across the road was deeper than Blair's rubber boots. Two more people have died and Blair has funerals tomorrow and the next day—that makes four in one week.

In hopes that the mailman will be out tomorrow I'll stop now.

With love to you all,

Greetings from the Island!

It looks like a lovely springlike Sabbath day, and my husband has just set off for church— on foot of all things. He's going to Glenwood, about three miles through the woods and then another mile or so along the road. This burst of energy is occasioned by the fact that this is the worst time of year to get anywhere—part of the roads are good for cars, other parts impossible, some roads are sleigh roads still and in others one can't possibly use a sleigh. And the men who have wagons have driven him so often that he decided to walk, and he's sure to get a drive back with one of the Glenwood people.

It's been a terrific week for Blair: A funeral Tuesday, and another one Wednesday which meant that Monday had to be spent in writing funeral sermons. And funerals take a lot out of you. So on Wednesday evening we decided that no matter what the roads were like we were going to take Thursday off and get away from here. So at nine-fifteen on Thursday morning we started. The car went very nicely after having been in the garage for two months nearly. The road between here and O'Leary wasn't too bad for it was early enough in the morning for it to be still frozen, but really it must have been frightful on some of the warmer days. We arrived at O'Leary and went at once to the garage. We had decided that if we could get a chance back to Springfield in the evening we would just leave the car in O'Leary to have it all overhauled or whatever is done to cars, and just leave it there until the week of Pine Hill Convocation, and all we would have to do would be get a lift into town by wagon, sleigh, truck or what have you, and we'd be all set. Anyway we went from O'Leary on to Summerside and Summerside seemed just like a metropolis—a huge place. Blair got our 49 license and we wandered all over the stores and ate in a restaurant, and it was a most enjoyable day. The funniest part of it was how many people we saw whom we knew in Summerside, all of them from Springfield. We kept running into our neighbors all day. Some of the congregation were in the Summerside hospital and so the minister made calls there, and we brought one of the men from Glenwood home in the car with us. Got back to O'Leary at about five and left the car there and came back here with the storekeeper who had also been in Summerside. And our activity had worn us out so completely that we went to bed at 8.30. But my, it was good to have that day off. And it really looks as though we may get to Halifax in another couple of weeks. We're beginning to talk of it, though still very cautiously.

Last week we bought a new radio. The battery on our portable was getting very weak again, and we figured that we just couldn't afford to keep getting new ones every month and a half or so. We bought it through the store here and got it at cost. A really nice little Marconi with a walnut case and long and short wave—and all the stations we can get on it, I've never known such reception before. And we decided that here a radio is not a luxury—it's an absolute necessity. Having got the radio the next problem was to get it connected, and to this problem Blair gave most of Friday, up on the barn roof putting up ariels (something wrong with spelling here) and rushing in and out of the house with wires. Well it goes now, and though I feel that there are an exorbitant number of wires in evidence all over the kitchen, it's worth it.

Oh yes, we put the new radio in the kitchen of course. That room has been our living room all winter and we're keeping closer to it than ever right now. Because for over a week now we haven't had to have a fire in the furnace. It's grand not to have the fire to wonder about and pamper, and we feel very free without it. But it means that the kitchen is much the most comfortable room in the house.

Two more wedding presents this week—a beautiful watercolor picture of the Prairie from Dr. and Mrs. A. B. B. Moore of Saskatoon and a wonderful afghan crotcheted (spelling again?) by my grandmother in Truro. This is in red and wine and black and looks very nice in the living room (not the kitchen).

This letter was interrupted while I went for the milk—say, it is a beautiful day, really warm for the first time. Now I wish that I had walked to church with my husband today. He couldn't have chosen a more ideal morning to walk.

Monday: Blair came home from Church, and then we had to rush to church here, back for supper and then he started out again, by sleigh this time, and I went to spend the evening with a neighbor and somehow this letter never got finished. It was late when we got in, and were we ever tired! Today being our day off we really took it in style, didn't get up til ten, and then Blair had to clean out the stove, and finally at eleven-fifteen, in a very sooty kitchen looking like two hoodlums, me in old slacks, three members of the congregation at Glenwood arrived in to pay a call. Very embarrassing—our reputation is probably ruined. We tried to be very charming and witty to take their minds off our condition and that of our kitchen—but I don't think we pulled much wool over their eyes.

Ah me—the life of public figures is a difficult one.

Love to all,

```
                              The Manse,
                              O'Leary R.R. 1
                              Prince Edward Island
                              April 10th.
```

Dear Folks;

Palm Sunday Morning, and Blair has just set off for Cape Wolfe in a
weird looking buggy affair, and I am thinking of you going to church in
Sydney and Ottawa—and, I hope, in Halifax (Oh, of course you will be,
exams are getting so near).

There seem to be many things I want to tell you in this letter, but
One Thing is so much more important than all the rest that I'll have
to tell it right now instead of sort of casually springing it on you in the
last paragraph. You see—we're going to have a baby. A new Colborne
is due into this world sometime in November. We're quite amazed by
the whole thing! So it is a very awed pair who are writing you today—I
know that this has happened to other people before, but when it's our
child, it seems so remarkable. On Friday we went into O'Leary and I
saw the doctor and he confirmed what we had suspected for some time.
We hope that you find the idea of becoming grandparents and aunt
and uncle even half as thrilling as we think the idea of being parents is.
Our blessed event will likely cause quite a stir in the community round
about here—and perhaps the rumours have even now started circulat-
ing. When we were in Summerside last week I decided to lay in some
supplies just in case—and I was wandering round Smallman's store
looking for a clerk and clutching a book entitled, "Knitting for Babies"
and various balls of pink and blue wool when of course I ran smack into
the people from the farm down the road, and blushed crimson! Anyway
that's our big news.

The question of whether we get to Halifax a week from tomorrow
or not is still unsettled. The car is still in the garage in O'Leary and new
parts have been ordered from Charlottetown but if they are unobtain-
able there they will have to send to Sydney for them, which means they
would not come in time. So we are just not counting on it—or trying not
to.

We had those wonderful people known as plumbers in here on Wednesday—and do you know—the water runs out of our sink now, for the first time since I arrived. It is the most wonderful luxury and now Blair doesn't have to spend his holy time emptying slop pails—and I can do a great deal of my washing in the sink.

We found an ice cream freezer in the store-room and so on Tuesday we decided to try our hand at homemade ice cream. We got cream from the lady across the road and I made the mixture while Blair hunted ice, chopped it up and turned the freezer and turned the freezer and turned the freezer, etc. Making ice cream is a lot of hard labor for someone— and it was his idea. But the finished product was really very good—except that a pint of cream makes quite a bit more than enough for two people. We had ice cream for supper and for lunch before bed and again the next day—I guess it wasn't terribly good for our figures—but what the heck, I'm losing mine anyway.

We had quite a trip into O'Leary on Friday. We had lots of chances to get a drive in that day for there was a progressive-conservative meeting on and everyone with any P.C. tinge at all was heading in that direction—and of course everyone was more than willing to take us in hopes that we might see the light. So we went in with Mr. MacDougall down the road right after lunch. The road wasn't too bad going in—but coming back it was terrific, deep, deep ruts in the mud—Mr. MacD. is an excellent driver, I think we would still be between here and town if he had not been so good. We were certainly glad that we were not in our own car. Knowing Blair you will realize that if there were a political meeting anywhere near where he was, he would be there regardless of which party happened to be holding it—so he went to the P.C. meeting. He did not get converted or see the light. And I am afraid that he disgraced himself: One speaker was introducing the candidate and said, "Brigadier Price was born in 1899 at the age of 16 (pause) he joined the army". Blair found the statement amusing and let out a great guffaw—which would have been all right except that he was the only one in the whole hall who saw the funny side. He also had to look at numerous movies of George Drew, which was very hard on him. We both had supper at the Dicksons and immediately afterwards left for Springfield.

This next week promises to be fairly busy, on Tuesday there is a concert at the community hall—all we have to do is attend. Then on

Thursday I entertain the Ladies Aid here at the manse—I'm not looking forward to it, but I'm not going to go to very much trouble. Friday is of course Good Friday and we're having service at each of the points and for a change I am going to preach.

```
             Lots of love from the expectant
             Colbornes,
```

Hello there, one and all,

Monday evening and the Colbornes are sitting as usual in their kitchen—Blair is planning out sermons for the next month, he now has the dates of the next five Sundays written down, I haven't noticed much else. But I'm glad that you can't see me, for here I sit all done up in bobby pins, curlers, etc., having spent all day receiving a home permanent. My hair was getting pretty grim, and when one of the girls from down the road came home from Prince of Wales College for the Easter holidays and mentioned to me that she had often done these things, I lined her up right away. So she came and stayed all day—and OH, the valuable community gossip I picked up! Blair was both fascinated and horrified by the whole proceeding. I don't know yet what the finished product will look like, but it feels nice and soft.

Last week was really terrific—very busy. On Tuesday evening we went to a concert put on by a group of the young people of the community in the hall here. It was quite an eye-opener in regard to this community in which we live and work. Liquor had been imbibed very freely before and during the performance by members of both audience and performers, and it was desperate—fights in the audience and some on the stage who had no idea whatsoever what they were doing. Springfield West is a place with a pretty grim reputation, and it really lived up to it on Tuesday night.

Then on Thursday night I entertained the Ladies Aid. As that was my first real entertaining job it was quite a strain. I had to have the house looking fairly decent, and then according to the rules, I had to have five different things to eat. So we planned, sandwiches, ritz biscuits with cream cheese and a slice of olive, brownies, macaroons and spice cake. Well things started going wrong early. We had to get our olives in O'Leary six days before we were to use them. I have always liked olives, but I have read that people in my "condition" get passions for certain kinds of food—well, I simply couldn't keep away from those olives, and in less than a day there wasn't one left. So we had to plan again. On Wednesday I made brownies and they were all right—on Thursday I started out in the morning with the cake, something I had tried and had luck with before, well, I did something to it and when I took it out of the pan it just broke up. Was I depressed? Then I tried the macaroons, I had never tried them before but my cookbook said, "When little children want to start cooking, let them start on these", so how could mine fail? I don't know but they ran all over the pan and looked most peculiar. Was I depressed? But, I thought, maybe I just think they look weird, I'll wait and see what Blair says about them—he took one look and turned to me and said, "What happened to them?" And I am ashamed to report that I burst into tears! However we found that they tasted delicious so we poked and pushed them round about so that they weren't quite so queerly shaped and used them anyway. And I made a chocolate cake in a giant rush and when the first guests arrived we were a very cool and collected host and hostess, and I took the ladies into the parlour, which was very surprised to have people sitting in it, and Blair had the men in the kitchen where he innocently suggested that they listen to the political speech over CBC—pretending that he hadn't known for a whole week that M. J. Coldwell was speaking. And at the end of the evening everybody said that I was a "lovely cook".

Friday was Good Friday and it again was Quite A Day, though in a different sort of way. I was doing the preaching for the family at all the churches that day. We went to Cape Wolfe in the morning—me and the man across the road in a wagon. It was a beautiful day sunny and clear and I enjoyed the trip very much. We went through the woods to get there and came back by the shore—Northumberland Strait was completely clear of ice as far as you could see and was blue as blue. We had good crowds out in all the churches, which was rather a surprise, but maybe they wanted to hear the "preacher's wife". I enjoyed the feel of a pulpit again. In the afternoon we went to Bethel Church right here—and in the evening to Glenwood—and that was the trip!! Just Blair and I went in the wagon with the safest and slowest old nag that I have ever come across. We thought that we would never get there—we talked to that horse and clucked at it and yelled at it and hit it and it would trot for about half a minute and then settle back to the slowest walk imaginable. We did get there—but getting home was a lot more difficult. Fog had come down and made the blackest night and the road was very muddy in places and we had no lantern, so we had to walk the animal the five miles home. We were rather glad to get back that night—to put it very mildly.

And Sunday was Easter, a cold miserable day. Church here in the morning and Blair preached a very good Easter sermon (I was proud of him!) and then we went out for dinner with a young couple in the congregation, and while I stayed and spent the afternoon with the wife, Blair and the man battered their way through the mud to Cape Wolfe by car. And in the evening one of the men took him by car almost to Glenwood and then went back and called for him after. So it looks as though next Sunday we will be able to use the car.

We're not going to be in Halifax for Pine Hill Convocation—in case some of you people there are looking for us—the car wasn't ready, and that trip by train is just too grim for any holiday at all. However next week when the car is ready we may take a little trip somewhere.

Bye for now—and thank you for remembering us at Easter.

with love,

Hello Again!

It's Tuesday evening, and I hope I can get this letter written while Blair is across the road helping one of the farmers with his income tax—he seems to be regarded as quite an expert on such things round here. Friday evening last we spent at one of the other homes while he straightened out that tax; last evening he helped me with mine and did his own this afternoon, so by the thirtieth we won't any of us have to disappoint Mr. Abbott.

Tomorrow afternoon Blair has a wedding—it is the first this year and really I think it is about time after all the funerals he's had. I've been invited too—and I'm most excited, it will be the first wedding we've been to since our own. So we'll get all dolled up for it. It is to be in a home, and we know both the young people who are getting married, and that makes it nicer.

On Thursday last we went to the community shower for this bride held in the community hall. Such an event is a painful occasion. <u>Everybody</u> was there, and we all sat in dead silence and watched this poor girl seated on a decorated chair on the stage while the gifts were handed to her and she had to look suitably pleased about them all—even when she received about forty glasses.

And speaking of showers, remember my speaking of the one they were planning to hold for us at Cape Wolfe which we never got to—and which I guess would have been very like the one mentioned above—just as painful—well at last the road is open from the Cape up to here and last week one of the men drove up and brought us our presents from the shower. We'd forgotten all about them so we were very surprised and pleased, especially since it meant that we would not now have to go through the ordeal of a shower. And the presents were wonderful—they gave us a chenille bedspread, just a <u>beauty</u>, white mostly, with delicate pastel colors. The presents came the night I had the Ladies Aid, so I put it on our bed immediately, and took it off immediately after they went home. Then they gave us a card table, a most useful thing to have, and it is a nice one too with pictures of horses all over it. And in addition individuals had sent presents, jars of chicken and lobster, home canned, and preserves of various sorts. So it was just like Christmas.

And to our surprise, just as we get to thinking that the honeymoon is over and the wedding presents have finally stopped coming (and after all it is about time—I finished knitting a jacket for the baby yesterday!)— suddenly we get some more. In the last week we received three more presents—a very nice mahogany tray from Elinor and Earl Leard, a long narrow one, grand for sandwiches; and from the Retsons of Truro a wonderful present, a desk set consisting of blotter holder and book ends in leather beautifully hand tooled by one of the Women in Truro; and finally, last but not least, a money order for <u>twenty</u> dollars from Mr. and Mrs. W. McT. Orr of Halifax. We've been speculating as to how we will use it constantly for the two days that we have had it. This is one present that I am very grateful did not arrive until after we had been married for a little time—for how would we ever have realized back in those idyllic days of singleness that what we would want most in life at the end of four months would be a copper bottomed frying pan with a lid!

We still are car-less, although by the first of this week all the parts were supposed to be here. Blair was in O'Leary on Friday to see about it. The difficulty is that now the frost is coming out of the O'Leary road, and everyone is getting stuck, who wants a car anyway? Just about a hundred yards from the manse there is the worst mudhole in PEI—for two weeks now there have been an average of six cars a day stuck there. It is a spot that has a never ending fascination for my husband, about three times every day he suddenly darts out the back door. When I yell at him where is he going (just checking up on him!) his answer is always, "Just wanted to see who's stuck in the mud hole now". However, in spite of the bad roads he went by car to the different points—one of the men took him and came back here for dinner afterwards. It was a miserable day, with high winds and rain and snow most of the afternoon. It wouldn't have been so bad if the weather forecast on Saturday night hadn't promised us the warmest day of the year!

We feel that there must be some more news—but can't think of any so we'll just sign off for this week—

with our love,

Joan

67   Joan Archibald Colborne

May 4th.

Dear Folks,

May came to the Island—and we just can't believe our weather. It isn't like spring anymore, it's just like summer. Our front field is green as green, and just in the last three days, and the lilac bush in front of the window over our sink is just bursting in to leaf. And yesterday a couple of the little girls from down the road who come in to "call" on us quite regularly brought us a big bunch of beautiful mayflowers. The fields have just dried up overnight and the farmers will start planting very soon. And, oh, what a difference it makes in the way you feel about life! All last month I was itching to get away—anywhere; this month I don't want to leave at all, because it might mean missing something of this very boisterous spring.

Just as well we don't want to go anywhere, for we are still car-less. It's over a month since we so much as saw our Nash. They haven't been able to get some part for it. We hope to have it for next Tuesday, for on that day Presbytery meets in Charlottetown. If our bus is not ready, then the lay delegate from the field will take us, but if we can drive then we will go down on Monday and stay overnight. It sounds wonderful. On Monday Blair started out visiting without the car—it was a bad day to go, desperately hot and humid with scattered showers. He arrived home just a wreck, covered with perspiration and a thick coating of dust with sore feet and a sunburn.

We've had two weddings since I last wrote, one last Wednesday and one about an hour and a half ago, and with great glee I have pocketed my first wedding fees. Last Wednesday it was a wedding at the home of the bride's parents, and it was really a very nice wedding. At about 3.15, the Colbornes looking very swish, he in his black suit and clerical collar and she in a tailored suit of slate blue gabardine, set off down the road, and thereby let the village know when the wedding was to be (they always try to keep it a dead secret, but always fail) we knew we were being watched from every house we passed. The wedding was very small, just the parents, grandparents and witnesses and a couple of friends, and we ate tons afterwards. But following the ceremony and the eating, history was made at Springfield—a chivaree was held in broad daylight, in the middle of the afternoon. Truckloads of people came in weird costumes, all masked, and they just took over the party. I find that one highlight of these institutions is throwing everyone in sight up into the air—so they threw up the groom and then the bride and then the bridesmaid and the best man, and waxing more daring they gave the bride's mother a good heave into the sky, then the groom's mother, and finally they turned on the minister, black suit, clerical collar and all. So it was quite an afternoon. The wedding this evening was here at the manse, which involves much more work on my part, for I have to get the place cleaned up and we rush through supper (at weddings somewhere else you can always eat enough to make supper-getting unnecessary) and the dishes afterwards. But our house really looked very nice and I felt proud of it. I'm all for more weddings, they give very nice fees here!

The Wednesday that we had the first wedding turned out to be Quite A Day. The Wilkinsons who have the store here invited us to go into O'Leary with them for the evening to see a one-act play and concert in the hall. So we went in at eight o'clock and sat in the <u>hardest</u> seats in the hall until 9.30 when the show finally started. The orchestra, Steve Getson and His Old Timers, had had carburetor trouble or something. The show was pretty punk. Afterwards we ran into a friend of Blair's and Wilkinson's, Ray Kennedy, and he took us all into the restaurant for food afterwards, and guess what the three men talked about—politics! What else is there to talk about these days? Anyway it was twelve thirty when we finally got back here. We just weren't used to such wild excitement, and were we ever weary.

Another wedding present came today—a beautiful cup and saucer from Mrs. Grant of Pine Hill. That means that I still have thank you letters to write, and last week I thought I had finished them all off. Just for fun then I counted them up and found that I have written one hundred and twenty seven thank you letters for wedding presents.

Last night we went visiting with Mr. and Mrs. Collicutt, our nearest neighbors. We went way down the shore road by Cape Wolfe and spent the evening at this home. There was an old lady there ninety six years old and still pretty sharp. She reads but doesn't wear glasses, and while it was explained to us when we went in that "Mama is a little hard of hearing" I'm willing to bet that mama didn't miss one word of what went on that evening.

Blair is having a Board of Stewards meeting tonight and later on I will feed them. Right now they seem to be arriving in droves and I am wondering if I have enough food. I think I had better say farewell to you now and make some more sandwiches.

with love,

Dear Folks,

    It's so long since I wrote one of these letters that I have almost forgotten how to type. What with housecleaning and then visitors, life just got too busy, but now life seems to be back to normal again so I will start in again.

    After the very long winter and spring, the parson and his wife have been having a hectic whirl of activity—comparatively speaking. Why, since I last typed a letter we have been to Charlottetown once, to Summerside three times, have seen two movies—and Blair has been to one political meeting. And aside from the two bedrooms upstairs I have the house cleaning all done and have made new curtains for the kitchen and pantry. And of course—Blair has had two more funerals.

    It was just wonderful having Mum and Dad and Budge here. I had been wanting for so long to show them the place—and they were all suitably enthusiastic about our house and the community. Indeed they were very surprised by it all. We had awful weather, cold and raw with plenty of rain all the time. But we had loads and loads of time for talking, which was what we had looked forward to most. Blair took Dad up to Alberton on business one day they were here, and last Tuesday we both went in to Summerside to take him to the train—and we took in a movie as well. On Thursday Mum and Budge left and we took them into Summerside as well and got some shopping done. Then I had to speak that night in Glenwood church at the WMS thankoffering service. On Friday we had to go to Summerside again—to go to the dentist and to take in a meeting on Vacation Schools at Trinity United Church. When we left here Friday morning it was nice and sunny, but when we got out of church that evening it was raining—but just how hard it was raining we didn't realize until we got on the road to O'Leary. We had gone about five miles when we realized that we should have never left Summerside, the rain was just beating down in sheets and you couldn't see a thing. And we began to think of that terrible road from O'Leary home, and we were pretty worried. It was midnight when we got to O'L., and we were going through it when to our great surprise we saw a light in the Dicksons' manse so we went in there and took shelter for the night and came out here early yesterday morning.

We've had the car now since a week Thursday evening, and have driven miles since that time. It certainly is not satisfactory yet and it has been worked over at the garage about six times since we got it out.

We have been eating rhubarb from our garden for some time now, and today we noticed that the blossoms on our apple tree are beginning to come out. And our fields are just covered with wild strawberry blossoms. And two weeks from tomorrow we leave for Conference—isn't it wonderful.

Bye for now,

With love,

Joan

```
                          The Manse,
                            O'Leary RR 1
                            P.E.I.
                              June 4th
```

Dear People,

It's Saturday evening, and as my husband labours on his sermon for
Pentecost Sunday, I am going to be useful too and get this letter written.
It may be a bit disjointed as he has a habit of always asking my opinion
of such and such a point in the sermon, whereupon a deep theological
argument inevitably follows. However, here goes!

The week started off rather flat after having visitors suddenly to be
just two of us in this big house—however it was nice to sit in one of the
two comfortable chairs in the kitchen again without feeling guilty because someone must be having to sit on the uncomfortable ones. And
of course there weren't as many dishes, which isn't the disadvantage
it sounds, as I never had to do them while the guests were here. And
we can listen to the radio, which is much more easily done when there
are two people in the room than when there are five! And we get much
more mail when the Archibalds aren't here than when they are. But
anyway we missed them because we had had such a <u>very</u> good visit with
them.

After our visit to the Dicksons at midnight last Friday night we made
up our mind to do something which we have been talking about for a
long time—to invite them out here for supper. So we asked them for
last night. Entertaining is still a very major operation with us and most
of the week was taken up with the various forms of preparation toward
having four guests for supper. We got all the sterling silver cleaned and
I dug out my best place mats, and we got silver butter dishes and salts
and peppers polished (really putting on the dog! But after all it was really the first chance we'd had to show off our things). I went over the
house from top to bottom, because Mabel Dickson is a scrupulous
housekeeper, the kind that always has a kitchen floor you could eat off—
if you wanted to, and I didn't want her to think that the new minister's
wife was a lazy housekeeper, which is true. We made up menus and
changed them, and on Thursday Blair drove into O'Leary with a long

grocery list, and spent most of June's money on the 2nd of the month! Friday was <u>hot</u>, and we were cooking a roast—at five o'clock Blair forcibly ejected me from the kitchen and ordered me to have a bath, which accomplished the miracle of making me feel and act just like a human being when our visitors arrived. We thought we had a very nice meal—a beautiful roast of beef, excellently chosen and carved by the parson and superbly cooked by the parson's wife, with roast potatoes and corn and celery salad. And we had a big fruit salad with everything in it for dessert and a cake and chocolate cookies. So now I don't feel guilty whenever I go past the manse in O'Leary. An amusing incident occurred when I was taking the roast from the oven—Jeannie Dickson, age eight, was watching every move, and when she saw the roast her eyes got very big and she said, "Ooh, real meat!" Poor ministers' children! Probably some day our children will embarrass us in some such similar way.

For the last three days they have been working on our strip of road, widening it a great deal and filling our driveway up with dirt and sod about six times a day. And the dust on the road now! It's terrific. So much dust is particularly trying as Blair took two days last week to clean the car—he washed it and polished and did all the windows, so that you would simply not have recognized the Nash. On Thursday evening—a beautiful evening, went for a drive after supper, up through Alberton and beyond, nearly to Tignish. It's the first time we have done that and it was grand—and I am sure that everyone must have noticed our shining car.

We have had quite a change in weather in this last week, at last it is getting warm and the days have felt really hot—today was almost uncomfortable. And then in the middle of the afternoon we had a terrible thunder storm—I've never seen anything like the way the rain and hail came down.

Our kitchen is looking very nice, we have moved in the couch and covered it with our red afghan and the result is a much nicer looking room—and also one where more than two people can sit in comfort.

We planted our garden last Tuesday. The only plowed land on the premises is a little patch about five feet by three, so we put in lettuce and radishes, and we rush out first thing every morning to see if the garden is up yet. This morning for the first time we saw little things which we think are radishes. Today also our lilacs are really bursting out. And we have discovered a little clump of narcissus that should be in bloom tomorrow. And the apple blossoms came out today. So we really feel like true householders as we go out every day and inspect our property. We have at least two tenants, too. Right down by our rhubarb patch in the vine that goes over the woodshed robins have built a nest, and the mother nearly goes mad every time we get rhubarb. We peeked in the nest and there are lovely blue eggs in it. And the swallows have nested in the barn. There seemed to be so many going in and out that we suspected it, and this morning we found the nest—a most amazing construction, made almost completely of mud and stuck plunk right on the side of a rafter.

Just a week from Monday and we go to conference—we're looking forward to it to say the least. Time starts going so fast once it gets to really be spring.

```
Must stop now-but love to you all
from both of us,
```

```
                            O'Leary R.R.  1,
                            P.E.I
                            June 11th,
Saturday Afternoon.

Dear People,
```

Blair is out visiting at the moment, and my house is tidied and my ironing is completed, and I have just had a lovely hot bath (Saturday, you know—and we have to have them about six hours apart if we are both to have hot water!) so feeling very clean and right with the world I proceed to write:

We've really had a very busy week, with visitors and meetings and preparations for our trip. We leave Monday and we will be away for a week, so Blair had to make plans for the services next Sunday. The Y.P.U. is taking the service at Glenwood and we had to look up material for them and type it all out and he had to visit all those taking part and see that they knew what to do. It's a lot more work than preaching yourself, but not unpleasant work for those taking part are three very attractive young girls (that's where he is this afternoon). He has done a lot of visiting this week. One morning he left at ten, dashed in and out again for lunch, and appeared next at seven thirty in the evening.

We have had car trouble twice this week—Sunday morning was the most dramatic time. Church was at Glenwood and at about 10.30 a.m. he went out to start the car and it wouldn't start. After trying for quite some time he went over to the neighbors, but both of our nearest neighbors on whom we always call in time of emergency were miles away looking for a lost calf. He came back and tried again—no luck, and it was getting later and later—so he set off racing down the road—dog collar and all looking for <u>anybody</u> with a car. At last he found someone and at three minutes to eleven he was hauled out of the yard and then the car started—but he was twenty minutes late for church. Then last night we were stuck in O'Leary till well after midnight because the car wouldn't start. It's a very queer thing, because the car is running just beautifully otherwise—but it is very disconcerting and annoying never knowing whether or not it will start.

We were very thrilled to have visitors last Sunday. And surprised too—for we had forgotten that it was a holiday weekend. At about two in the afternoon the Murdoch MacLeans from Sydney arrived (Blair's aunt and uncle and two cousins—for readers who do not know). They hadn't seen the place before and so I was thrilled to be able to show them all over it. I don't think there is anyone Blair likes a good long talk with so much as Murdoch, and I just about had to push him out the door to get him to church—and I still don't know whether the MacLeans got the boat or not, so many discussions between the two men took place before Murdoch's family could get him away. We had a very good visit with them and were so pleased to see them.

We had lots of meetings during the week—Blair had a meeting with the church treasurer on Monday night; I entertained the Women's Institute here on Tuesday night—it was a very poor night and only four turned out, and the house got so cold that we had to meet in the kitchen, while Blair sat in the parlour encased in sweaters. On Wednesday night we both went to Glenwood for Young Peoples. On Thursday I went to Ladies Aid, while Blair went with Ray Collicutt from across the road to a Liberal meeting in O'Leary to hear Mr. Mayhew the Minister of Fisheries—he said it was a real good meeting. Then on Friday night we both went into O'Leary to the CCF meeting—after which, as a judgment upon us, I am afraid, the car wouldn't start. But it was a real good meeting, just as big as the Liberal one, and very enthusiastic.

On Friday evening before the CCF meeting we had a very honoured visitor—F. R. Scott, Professor of Constitutional Law at McGill and one of the leading modern Canadian poets, I had even studied his poetry in one of Professor Burns Martin's classes. The man is also the National Chairman of the Cooperative Commonwealth Federation party, and it was in this latter capacity, not as professor or poet that he visited the Island and the Colbornes. They happened to come down here because the Provincial Secretary and Organizer of the CCF is a friend of Blair's, and I guess they had some time before the meeting in O'Leary. And that poet sat at our kitchen table and on this very machine on which I reverently type now, typed out a report of his speech for the Guardian (which they probably won't publish).

So all in all it has been a full week—and our lilacs are in full bloom, and our radishes are up, and we caught a rat in the store room and we entertained a poet—now I ask you, what people live a more exciting life than do we?

Love to you all,

Joan

Dear Families,

It is three months to the day since I typed my last letter to you. I fear that this famous book that we are going to write will have large gaps in it. But then I think people are getting tired and sick of books about ministers anyway. However, at last I must get busy on these strange epistles again, because, looking at it from a purely selfish standpoint they are fun for us to have.

And so we are back in the Manse on the Island. After a wonderful holiday, we really got back in earnest. Back to our clogged chimney and that water system and piles of dirty clothes, and SUCH a dirty house (by the way, have you ever seen nice ripe bananas at the end of five weeks—Blair very thoughtfully left a half dozen of them here when he went away and they had made quite an impression on the drawer in which they were left and upon the whole atmosphere of the kitchen). But it's really awfully good to get back—in spite of all—to be back in our own house again, and even being back to work feels sort of good after the first shock wears off.

We have been having us quite a clean up campaign (that is, clean up of everything but ourselves, for every evening that we have felt like a bath since coming back, that Water System has refused to co-operate—so we are a wee bit grimy)—I have been working on the first and second floors of the house while Blair has been working on the barn and basement and coal bin. We needed to do something, for a great deal of wild life moved in while we were away. Spiders have spun their homes in every corner, and the place was just overrun with crickets, we have squashed hundreds of them, and Blair's policy is "Squash them and leave them", which makes the linoleum look grand. Flies were thick here for the first couple of days, and we had weevils in the flour bin, and a rat in the basement. We are Not Alone. But the great mystery in our wild life exhibit came night before last and still has us puzzled. At about nine o'clock we were sitting peacefully in the kitchen when Something flew in from the dining room flew round the room and flew out the dining room door again. And it was a thing with a wing span of about four inches. While I sat in fear and trembling in the pantry Blair searched the whole house twice for it, and from that moment we have seen no sign of it. There was no way for it to get in and no way for it to get out—and we don't even know what it was. Blair says a swallow, but I hold out strongly for a bat.

However, now the house is fairly clean (except for the study which I firmly refuse to enter), and after a succession of washes there are almost no dirty clothes about. I got a little over zealous yesterday about laundry. It was a lovely sunny warm day and I decided to finish up my pile of laundry. I admit that my husband told me three times that it was no day to wash. I did. It just took the clothes about fifteen minutes to dry, but unfortunately we were getting the tail end of some hurricane and it took just about three minutes for every article on the line to get knotted up and wound in and out of the lines—worst mess I've ever seen. The minister had to spend the better part of half an hour untangling each thing separately—and I betcha there wasn't a neighbor in miles that missed the spectacle. I distinctly heard him mutter as he went back to his study, "You don't even deserve to escape with your life".

On Thursday Blair went to Presbytery which met in Summerside. He brought me home a present—a dust pan with a long handle so that you don't have to stoop down to scoop up your sweepings. Well, they are wonderful, and if any of you women are trying to keep house without them—don't, for they only cost 45 cents and are truly a revolutionary piece of household equipment.

On Friday we had visitors—and were we ever glad to see them! Earl and Elinor Leard and Howard and Dorothy Christie with young Robert age six months dropped in for an hour or so during the afternoon. We just sat and talked. I felt quite proud of my husband, he hadn't shaved, but on top his head he had about five times as much hair as Earl, Howard and Robert put together. We hope to run up to Cascumpec tomorrow or Tuesday to see the Leards again. They leave here on Thursday and sail for England from Quebec on Friday, and will spend a year there before going to India—so dear knows when we'll have a chance to see them again. We are thinking of going down to the Christies on the 19th of this month to stay overnight. We have to go down to Summerside that day for I have a dentist appointment, then we will go on through to Hunter River. They have a lovely baby.

While I have been writing this two cars have been going round and round the house. One is ours and the other Ray Collicutt's. Because when we got in the car to go to church this morning, guess what—It wouldn't go! Even the starter didn't make a sound. Why does it ALWAYS pick Sunday to happen? It is going now so they are trying it out by going round and round. We are hoping that this doesn't happen two months from today, November 11th!

It sure is beginning to feel like fall around here—it was really cold last night and we were glad of a fire on in church this morning. The farmers have just about finished threshing, and potato digging will start in a little over a week—how very quickly a season goes. We have been getting gifts of vegetables from many people, which we certainly appreciate, and on Thursday one of the men brought us a whole truckload of wood as a present.

Blair has just come in from church at Cape Wolfe. The rumours are starting already—one woman dashed up to him when he got to church to inquire for me, said that she had heard in O'Leary Saturday night that I had been taken to the hospital on Thursday. People must have started counting months at that news!

Bye for now,

with love from both of us,

Howdy Folks,

Well, here it is Sunday again and time for the way down east news from the Colbornes. Nothing very thrilling or exciting in the Island news, but such as it is, here it is.

You may not believe it, but Blair went out this morning and the car wouldn't go! Just exactly like it was last Sunday, dead as a doornail. And it has just gone like a top every other day during the week. I would advise all ministers never to buy cars from Roman Catholic priests, because I'm almost beginning to believe that our car definitely objects to going to Protestant service on Sunday. We had to be towed out the lane and down the road before it started—this is getting to be quite a Sabbath procedure. And now Ray and Verne Collicutt are scared to leave the district on Sunday for fear the minister will be stuck.

There seems to have been a lot going on this week. On Monday we went into O'Leary shopping (the people who run the store here were away on holiday). Then on Tuesday we made plans to go up and see Earl and Elinor Leard—however, we didn't get there. One of the women of the community came in with a tale of woe in the morning about how she absolutely had to get in to Summerside that day and had tried everybody in the community and couldn't get anybody to take her, so would Blair. He's sort of good natured and she seemed stuck so he agreed to take her. They didn't get back till after six, and he was fuming because when they arrived in S'side they met three different cars from within a mile of here. From now on we run no taxi service except in the case of birth, sickness, or death.

Elinor and Earl left the Island on Thursday and sailed for England on Friday, so on Wednesday we decided to go up to Leards and bid them a short farewell. They were just about finished all their jobs and packing, so we stayed most of the afternoon and had a grand visit with them. We all drove into Alberton during the afternoon. They invited us for supper, and while I was just dying for a meal out, it was going to be their last meal with their family for six and a half years, so we definitely declined. I mentioned in my last letter that we were planning next week to go and visit the Howard Christies the day we went up to Summerside—but unfortunately that is out because that same day they are having a bunch of relatives and we would have to sleep on the floor.

We are going to have an overnight guest a couple of weeks from today. Doctor Catherine Whittier, a missionary on furlough from India is visiting West Prince County over that weekend and is to preach at Bethel Church that Sunday morning. So I invited her to spend Saturday night here, and she is going to. It should be very nice having her.

We had a wedding here on Thursday afternoon, a horrible wet dismal afternoon—but it was a wedding, and they are sure nice things to have. Warren Dickson took one while we were away that we would otherwise have had, and told us with a great gleam in his eye that it had been a ten dollar wedding! Was I mad that we had to miss it. There are rumors round and about that there is to be a big church wedding up Glenwood way in October—but one party is Presbyterian and one United Church so the sixty-four-dollar question is, who is going to get it. I'm afraid that this sounds very mercenary—but then we kind of are, and weddings are nice anyway.

Aside from a couple of wet days the weather has been beautiful since we came back, clear sunny warm September days. It is a grand time to be living in the country, and the Island is really lovely right now. Just for fun I borrowed "Anne of Green Gables" the other day and I've been reading it through again. I find I still love it and Blair is going to read it next. To be living on the island and not to be acquainted with Anne is a very poor thing. But you know I'm shocked—the book was written in 1908 (at least it was published then, I guess it was written a while before that) and the Island has not changed one bit since that time, it could just as well be written about today round here. L. M. Montgomery's husband used to be the Presbyterian minister at Glenwood.

Tomorrow we go to Summerside, and we are hoping while there to do some shopping. We really are not very well prepared for our approaching guest (and I do not mean Dr. Whittier). We have set aside the blue room upstairs and we call it the nursery, but the only thing we have in it is a roll of cotton batten. We could keep the child in a bureau draw-er if we had a bureau drawer which we haven't, so we will get a basket for it and have a look at cribs. We both feel that we don't know just what we should get.

I was planning in this letter to tell you about how grand our stove has been since we got a new chimney. But I don't think I will for for the last half hour it has been very ornery and I have been struggling with it. Now at last it seems to have decided to burn. But it has been such an improvement on the way it used to be that I give thanks daily.

Poor Blair has just come in from the afternoon service and is leav-ing immediately for Alberton to make a hospital visit before the evening service. One of the kids on the field had an accident on Friday when a milking machine exploded and he was burned quite badly. Tomorrow is out for visiting so it seems that Blair must call today.

```
Well, that's all for now,

    With our love,
```

Dear People,

To Sydney, Ottawa, Halifax and Toronto our letter from the Island goes this week—we're really covering the country! We hope that you're all getting comfortably settled in for the winter. The vine up the side of our house is turning red, and there is that blue clarity about the air that means fall, and everybody is talking about potato digging, so winter isn't very far away.

To tell our story this week in the usual manner, I shall say, it is Sunday again, and when Blair went to start the car this morning there wasn't a sound from it at all. And that's true, though we couldn't believe it this morning, and I nearly decided not to tell you because it sounded just like the sort of thing I might make up. On Monday Blair had a new battery put in the car, on Thursday he had the car lights fixed, and he used the car every single day last week, including Saturday, and she just went like a top. But this morning, as soon as it saw Blair coming in that clerical collar, it wouldn't budge. So the poor Collicutts had to come rushing to the rescue again, and service at Cape Wolfe was three minutes late. It's just so awfully silly—and as Budgie says, What do you bet young Amos will decide to arrive on the Sabbath Day?!

On Monday we went to Summerside quite early in the morning. I had a dentist appointment—one of those quite unbelievable ones when it turns out there is nothing that needs doing to your teeth. Then we shopped. I think that was a mistake—if we do it too often it might break up our happy marriage. It so turns out that Blair's idea of shopping is to go into a store, see what you want, buy it and leave. Now me, I look at a thing in one store, but I'm not ready to make up my mind, I want to see what they are charging for the same thing in the store down the road. It involves much footwork, and we really covered Summerside. I am confounded that a man who is so patient about such annoying things as our car and our water system, can get so cheesed off about such a little thing as his wife's shopping. But when we got home we discovered that in about three minutes he had bought more things than I had all after-noon! He had a new khaki shirt and khaki work trousers, and a horrible steel brush for cleaning out the inside of the furnace, and an interesting bottle of some concoction for taking the sediment away from the inside of the kettle. I had a clothes basket to keep the baby in and a little mat-tress to go in it and a rubber sheet and a mirror so that Dr. Whittier will be able to see herself next weekend. But my, I had seen a lot!

Other events during the week included a visit to our M.L.A. here over a relief case that is quite a problem, and Blair took in a local auc-tion down West Point way, and according to his reports <u>everybody</u> was there. He ordered a mail box on Thursday in town with United Church Manse on it instead of U.C. Parsonage, probably the old Methodists will be mad, but the mailman won't care what is on it, he will be so thankful to see a new box—ours hangs at such a peculiar position now, that one rainy day during the week in an effort to get the mail in without get-ting out of the car that he ran right into the ditch and stuck fast in the mud and had to get hauled out. I've had a number of visitors during the week—it is very interesting, by November 11th I believe that I will know the case histories of every pregnancy and confinement that has taken place in Springfield, Glenwood and Cape Wolfe in the last few years.

On Thursday night Blair had to go into Alberton to a Young Peoples Executive meeting for the Presbytery or something. It was a miserable pouring wet night (as they all were last week except Saturday) and as I didn't relish the thought of staying home alone he left me in O'Leary and went on and I spent the evening with Mabel Dickson. It was very nice as I hadn't seen much of Mabel for some time, so I took my knitting and we spent the evening chatting in their kitchen. When young Norma Dickson saw me she said, My goodness Joan, you're getting terribly fat! They sit in the kitchen all the time, and they have only one chair that is even the least bit comfortable, and it sits always right alongside the stove so that you can only sit on it for very brief intervals without get-ting par boiled. It was sure nice to get back to our kitchen, in which we now have three big comfortable chairs—which actually doesn't leave us much room to do anything else but sit in the kitchen. When we got home that evening we found that an old, almost forgotten friend had re-turned. There was unmistakable evidence that a skunk had been roam-ing through our woodshed in our absence.

During the last week I have done something which is quite new for me. I have become a pickler—not through choice, but really through necessity, because people give you things, and you can't waste them. The first week we were here the famous Mrs. Frizzle gave us a half a citron, she gave it to Blair with instructions that I was to make preserve out of it. I had never seen nor tasted a Citron before and had no idea what to do with it, and there was not a citron mentioned in either of my cook books—so it sat around and I forgot to ask people what to do with it. Finally one day Mrs. Collicutt was in and I remembered to ask her, so the next day with the best of intentions I reached for my half citron, only to find that a ripe citron does not keep indefinitely and that this was far beyond the useable stage. And I know that the next time I see Mrs. F she will ask about my citron preserve—and what will I say? So it must not happen again. Last week our next door neighbours, the Rixes brought us a grand basket of vegetables including more beets and Cucumbers than we would ever need, then the next day the Livingstones from Glenwood brought us a big box of green tomatoes. So we blew ourselves to a dozen pint jars, and I collected pickle recipes from all and sundry and we bought onions and vinegar—and now there are nineteen bottles of pickles on our pantry shelf—pickled beets and mustard pickles and chow. And am I ever proud when I look at them! they are very much in the way there, but I keep thinking someone may come in, and I will wave nonchalantly at my nineteen jars and say, "Oh, I've just done a little pickling." I should say, "We have done some pickling," because certainly I had much help from my husband. You should have seen us sitting here at the kitchen table Friday night getting the ingredients ready for the chow, we chopped hundreds of tomatoes and then started on the onions, and wept copiously. But it was kind of fun, and I was amazed at how little work it was.

Our Thought for the Week is this: In spite of all that we hear on the radio, it is still very difficult as we trot upstairs to bed each night, each clutching our kerosene lamp, to believe that we really live in the Atomic Age.

With our love,

Joan

O'Leary R.R. 1
P.E.I.
October 6th

Greetings—

Our Sunday afternoon letter seems a little late this week—or is it next Sunday afternoon's letter arriving a little early? I haven't quite decided yet. Anyhow—all last week and Sunday especially was a constant stream of visitors and our letter writing time was cut to nil. But today we are through lunch very early and Blair is off to Glenwood visiting, so I will endeavour to get this letter written—but I'm willing to bet that I have visitors before I get it finished. Perhaps people think of me as a sort of invalid, in any case, I seem to be down on everybody's visiting list this week or so.

Our visitors have come from all over the field—sometimes at very opportune times, sometimes at most inopportune ones. Last week two of the women from Glenwood came most opportunely—I had slaved all morning and I had the kitchen floor scrubbed and waxed and a big batch of bootheels (soft molasses cookies) made when they arrived right after dinner—so I didn't have to try to keep their eyes off the floor all afternoon and I was able to serve tea and bootheels. After they had gone Blair and I sat back and congratulated ourselves: Wasn't it lucky I had the floor scrubbed, said I. Yes, and wasn't it fortunate that I shaved this morning, said the man of the house. It certainly was, I agreed. And wasn't it good that I had made cookies. Blair agreed, and then a funny look came over his face. But wasn't it too bad you didn't wash your knees before they came? And I looked down and sticking out from a short skirt were two bare legs topped by the <u>filthiest</u> pair of knees I have ever seen!   .

Blair has taken up a new job—furniture repairing. We have been wondering what to put the baby's things in to. They are piling up on beds and chairs and things upstairs and there isn't an empty drawer in the house—and we were getting sort of desperate. Then we located an old cupboard in the woodshed and dug it out. It looked pretty hopeless at first but he got busy on it and after taking off layers and layers of paint, we find that we have a pretty good thing. It is hand made and very old—there are no nails used in it, just wooden pegs. A couple of coats of paint and we'll really be set.

Last week, no, this week—we got our first mail order off to Eatons—the result of about a month's study of catalogues. We ordered baby sheets and flannelette and diapers and other things, and now we are sitting round in great excitement waiting for our order to come. And having sent our first order off day before yesterday, we got our second one off today. I hope it doesn't get to be too much of a habit.

Last weekend, you will remember we were to have Dr. Catherine Whittier, a missionary from India as a guest. She was our first overnight guest apart from our families and you don't really count, so it was quite an occasion for us. We wanted everything to be as nice as possible and on Thursday and Friday I cleaned the house. Saturday morning I woke up and before I was even half awake I knew it—we had had a visitor during the night, and even up in the bedroom with the window closed (my husband is not a fresh air fiend) I could smell skunk. One of those dear little animals had managed to get into our basement. It was a good blowy day and Dr. Whittier arrived at the front door rather than the back and I don't think she even noticed until next morning when we went out back to go to church. We had expected her to arrive Saturday evening but she appeared on Saturday afternoon at three o'clock just as I was sinking exhaustedly into bed after baking for her all morning. We kind of enjoyed her visit—although we both agreed that she was a very strange person—but she did have the most magnificent appetite. Feeding her was pure joy. (Luckily I was prepared.)

I am glad to report that on Sunday morning the car started up pronto without any difficulty at all. Our report on the pump is not so satisfactory. We have not been able to get the water pumped up high enough to have a bath since the first week we arrived home. So we each had one bath in September—but be not dismayed, we did have sponge baths. Blair has been trying regularly to get the plumber from Summerside, he calls him every time he goes into O'Leary, and he actually got a promise that he would come out last Monday. No one appeared. Plumbers are a little like angels and archangels, you may believe that there are such things—but you don't expect to see them.

Last evening we went down Cape Wolfe way for a baptism. It was very nice. We were invited for supper first, and had a big supper. After dishes were cleared away we sat and talked for a while (men and women separately, of course). Then they brought in the little two months old baby and put on the christening dress that her sister and brother and father had worn too, and in the lamplight in the nice warm kitchen Blair baptized the baby.

We were thrilled yesterday to have a letter from the Howard Christies to say that they had been promised a duck for thanksgiving, and would we come down and have thanksgiving dinner with them and stay as long as we liked. Well, would we ever! Thanksgiving always seems like a holiday when you want to do something special, and when it is both of our birthdays as well it would be horrible to just sit home. So we are going down Monday and we will stay over night.

I had my second last visit to the doctors day before yesterday. I'm to go in again toward the end of the month, "ten or twelve days before your confinement", says he. Gosh. Gosh. The more active life round here seems to be agreeing with me, for I don't have to take anymore pills until the last couple of weeks, and I have lost five pounds in the last month which pleases him—and me, greatly.

Well that seems to be all the news for now—and it is only quarter to three and there have been no visitors, and I think I will go to bed (and now the visitors are sure to come).

Love to you all from both of us

Joan

Hello Everyone—

Blair and I have just been going over the events of our life since the last letter—and there seems to be so much to say about this exciting life that we lead that it seemed wise to start this letter tonight as it would likely take all day tomorrow to write it!

We last wrote on Thursday—well on Friday we were invited to a farewell party given by some of the church people for one family on the field up West Point way who are moving into O'Leary. A presentation was to be made to them, and Blair was joed for the job which so often falls to ministers, that of making the presentation speech. Well, no sermon was ever worried about as that speech was and I listened to and contributed jokes and stories all the week before in order that he could find just the right story to preface his remarks. Such agony! However in the end you will be relieved to know that he did his task very well—and his story was very funny. It was a much better than average shower, everybody didn't sit round and look uncomfortable, instead we played games and had a lot of fun. We did charades and twenty questions—and guess what I stumped them on—potato bug. It so turned out that it was good we went to the shower in more ways than one. We had had a further Frizzle experience the day before. To buy wood round here is a pretty tough problem and back at the end of July Blair had ordered his winter's wood from Mr. Frizzle. On Thursday Mrs. F. apologetically informed us that they had only enough wood for themselves. So we were really out on a limb, for everybody with wood to sell has sold it. And at the shower we discovered that these people who are moving have a whole wood pile they are anxious to get rid of. So we sure grabbed it fast (figuratively speaking, of course). So now we will be warm this winter.

Saturday was a Great Day because we opened our birthday presents. Even though it wasn't either of our birthdays. And we certainly did well. We got half a dozen egg cups, the kind with a little part and a big part you know, so that now we won't have to use napkin rings for our eggs.

And a bureau scarf, and a baby's blanket with blue teddy bears on it. I got nice feminine things—a beautiful pair of sheer silk stockings, and perfume, and nice smelling soap and a compact. Blair got a huge pair of fur gauntlets and the most superb red plaid shirt (it was hardly opened before it was on), and a beautiful pair of hand knit socks (from me) and last but not least, a flannelette night gown! Then we got two cakes—one arrived last week and one this week, so nicely spaced that it must have almost been planned. Just as I was deciding this morning that I simply must do some baking, in came another cake. On that Saturday even though people didn't realize that it was our birthday they acted as though they did. Blair went out visiting in his plaid shirt (well, it was more businessing than visiting) and came home with a bag and a big box. I rushed out and looked in them—the bag was full of mushrooms, some of them big as saucers and that is no exaggeration. When I stuck my nose into the box I was confronted by eight live lobsters. And the day before we had bought a roast, and we were going away on Monday. We had so much food in the house—it's always either a feast or a famine. But they all tasted good—although we discovered that to kill, cook and open lobster sort of lessens one's appetite for it.

Sunday was the 75th anniversary of Bethel United Church here in Springfield and special services were held in the afternoon and evening. Mr. Fitzpatrick the minister at Alberton preached at the afternoon service, and then came back here to supper. After supper Blair drove him back to Alberton and then went on to Miminegash to take the evening service for the man who was taking our anniversary service in the evening. Certainly if crowds are any indication, our services were a success. In the evening especially the church was packed—and was it ever hot!

Monday was Thanksgiving Day and the beginning of a whole week of the most perfect autumn weather. It was just the kind of a day that Thanksgiving Day should always be. We started out from here at about 9.30 to do the 65 mile drive down to Hunter River. The trees were just a blaze of colour and the sky was a brilliant blue—and they had even fixed the worst section of the pavement—so we had a wonderful drive down. Got to the Christies in time for a good duck dinner, and we left Tuesday afternoon after dinner, and had a very good time. They have a beautiful manse and a lovely baby about six months old. They have absolutely everything for their baby, two sizes of cribs, a collapsible bath, high chair, pram, play pen, etc and etc. When I looked around I figured that

they must be bloated plutocrats, and then they told us that they hadn't
had to buy a thing for the baby, everything they had had been lent them
by sisters and brothers who weren't using those things at that time. We
felt pretty let down when we realized how little help Budge and Ed are
going to be along that line—however we'll be big about it and lend you
our clothes basket when you need it.

We came back through Summerside and stopped there for about
an hour, in the course of which time we got rid of over fifty dollars. We
bought a crib and mattress out of our carefully hoarded fifty-cent pieces.
And Blair got himself outfitted for the winter with a snow suit—no he
tells me it is called a flying suit. It is old air force stock about two inches
thick all over with a fur collar and should be wonderfully warm for those
sleigh rides. We got home at about 6.30 and Blair rushed over next door
to see if we had received any mail. We had asked the woman next door
to collect ours if there was any when she got hers. Well the poor soul.
There were three huge parcels including a twenty-dollar order from
Eatons and a box of books from the United Church which must have
weighed 30 lbs. Also magazines and papers and letters. We felt frightfully guilty—but my, it was a grand mail!

Wednesday marked <u>the</u> big social event in these here parts, and a
big event in our lives—Blair's first church wedding. He had a rehearsal
on Tuesday night and before he went we went over all the etiquette of a
church wedding to the best of our knowledge—but when he came home
and said that I should have been there because there was a flower girl
and he hadn't known what to do with her at all, I realized that this was
going to be some wedding. And it was—there were two bridesmaids as
well as the f.g., and ushers and the wedding party's dresses were beautiful. And it was in the middle of potato picking but <u>everybody</u> was there,
crowded into the Glenwood church—even the men. It was only the
third wedding in the history of the church and much the most elabo-
rate. We heard about one woman from up the road here whose husband
objected to her leaving the potato fields and she replied—If I don't get
to that wedding this afternoon, I'll never pick another potato as long
as I live. She got to the wedding. Blair is a most satisfactory marry-er. I
always feel so proud of him. We went to the reception afterwards—we
thought we would get a cup of tea and a sandwich, but no, fifty people
sat down at once to a huge supper of chicken and ham and salads and
dessert, and at our table alone there were ten different kinds of cakes.

So it was quite a time. We hope that such a public wedding will give many other people the idea—just the idea of getting married. Because we—especially me—like it so.

Remember I mentioned that elusive character, the plumber, in a previous letter? Blair went in to see him in Summerside on Tuesday and got no satisfaction from him at all. We were most depressed and figured that we wouldn't likely have a bath till spring. I discovered that Blair had said incidentally that there was always someone home (me). So we both went to the wedding on Wednesday—and the plumber came. Luckily he turned out to be a persistent man once he appeared and he had removed the lock from the back door, and gone to it and fixed the pump. It is wonderful now, pumps the water almost noiselessly, and I am happy to report that we are now both clean and fresh and sweet smelling.

Blair spent Thursday in the potato fields—and he has been groaning ever since. And we went out for supper on Friday night—and to bed at 8.15 last night, which evening this letter was started. And so ends another week.

Nicest thing that happened to me last week: I was in Holman's trying to get cotton stockings for the baby. The clerk showed me the smallest size and I said that even they seemed quite large. "Well," she asked, "how old is the baby?"

Nicest thing that was said about Blair: I had put out a wash on a chilly day and he brought it in for me. A little seven-year-old boy was watching from next door and he turned and said to his older sister, "My the minister sure is good to his woman".

You've certainly had enough from us for today, so bye for now,

Love.

Joan

```
                              The Manse,
                          O'Leary R.R.  1.
                          P.E.I.
                              Oct 23rd,
```

Dear People,

   This letter on this Sunday should be just the opposite of that lengthy
epistle which we sent out last week—for there seems to be so little to say
that I don't think that I can even fill <u>one</u> page. But acting on the hope
that a half page is better than nothing, I shall carry on. And yet it has
been a busy week and both of us have been on the go most of the time—
especially Blair. And he vows that in the course of it he has gained quite
a bit of muscle and lost a bit of tummy—as for me, well I just seem to
have gained quite a bit of tummy.

   The keynote of the week was WOOD—remember I told you that we
decided to buy the wood pile? Well, I don't think we realized just how
much wood that pile contained—Blair and Verne Collicutt have been
going after it all week in a huge truck, and the woodshed is full to the
roof right now and there is still over a truckfull left to be hauled here.
Piling it should keep the parson occupied during most of winter. Monday dawned—a perfect washday, and did I ever have a wash, so I got
all ready to wash while Blair made arrangements about getting wood
hauled. But just as the wash was to go into the tub he remembered that
the truck couldn't go under the clothesline, so I would have to wait
until the truck had been and gone. And do you know what time they
arrived to go for the wood—four thirty in the afternoon! As Blair would
say—was I cheesed off.

   Blair is the Christian Education representative to Presbytery for this
end of the Island and he has been busy arranging for the visit of one
of the field secretaries up here the first week in November, and it has
meant a lot of letterwriting and telephoning for not only does he have
to arrange meetings, but also accommodation because it is the logical
thing that he should stay here, but it happens to be the week before I am
supposed to go to the hospital, so I'm darned if I'll have him. We went
into O'Leary on Tuesday, Blair to telephone, me to shop. The Dicksons
invited us there for dinner, and I had a chance to have a real good visit

with Mabel. She sent us home with a dozen fresh rolls and an offer to take the field secretary off our hands—for both of which we were very grateful.

On Wednesday Blair decided that in spite of all the wood that needed piling, the great heap of coal out in front of the house that needed shovelling, the study that needed tidying—it was time to do some visiting. So we left in the morning and he took me to one of the homes on the field and parked me there for the day. He visited before dinner and then came back to this home for dinner then got right off again after and visited until suppertime. It was a very good arrangement as I am not keen on being left alone for long periods of time, so I just took my sewing and didn't have to get any meals all day—and we left with two huge cabbages, a can of chicken, a can of tomato and a can of plums, and a beautiful pink set of jacket, bonnet and bootees which the girl of the house had crocheted for our baby. So the people really were quite good to us!

On Thursday Blair drove George Wilkinson's truck down to Summerside—also George Wilkinson's wife (G.W. is the storekeeper and the prosperous man in the district). We had been thinking that if anything went wrong with our car on The Day (or The Night) we would call on George to drive us in as he has the newest, the smoothest car around. Therefore it seemed excellent policy to drive Mrs. Wilkinson to Summerside. Blair put in a good day there, visiting a couple he knew at Fort Massey YPU in Halifax who live out at the Summerside airport. The woman is a trained nurse and has had two babies at the Summerside hospital—she gave us the very heartening information that the equipment and the care there is excellent.

On Friday Blair and Verne piled wood all morning and all afternoon. My husband was a wreck at the end of the morning—he didn't think he could go back for the afternoon load, but then he seemed to get into his stride and came home at the end of the day full of vim and vigor and energy. Why I don't think we went to bed until almost nine o'clock.

Sometime during this last week I had just a passing thought that went like this, We've been back a month and a half and there hasn't been a funeral yet. I must guard against thoughts like that—for on Thursday one of the women at Glenwood died and the funeral was yesterday—and yesterday morning Blair went into O'Leary (at 7.30 a.m., believe it or not) to catch the morning train with mail and while there found out that one of the men at Cape Wolfe had died very suddenly, so he had to dash out to Cape Wolfe before dinner. And the funeral may be this afternoon—they haven't let him know yet. Anyway after supper Saturday evening he sat down to figure out what he would preach on today—his first moment to think all week!

Somewhere in between this round of activity he found time to get our new crib from O'Leary and get it set up in the "nursery". And also to renew our warfare on the mice and rats. We caught five mice in three days last week—the rats are a bigger problem. They got into our store-room in the woodshed and just about demolished our store of apples, potatoes and other vegetables which we had been saving for the winter. On Monday morning we will set out rat poison and see what happens.

The weather continues to be beautiful—and the car is just purring along—and both of us are very well—and I have written a whole page more than I should have—so we will bid you farewell for now....

with love,

Joan

The Manse,
O'Leary R.R. 1,
P.E.I.
Oct. 30th

Dear folks,

October 30th—that date means a lot of things: ten months ago we were married; Twelve days from now is supposed to be another Big Day. And finally, as I write this, I am cooking my first chicken. If the train of thought gets incoherent it is just because I am dashing up at intervals to gaze into the oven at our bird. I'm still not quite sure how I came to buy a chicken. I went to O'Leary on Friday and while there some women were talking about how much cheaper chicken was than meat (just 30 cents a pound here) and how long it lasted and suddenly I found myself buying one, so that I surprised my husband when the time came to go home with a chicken complete with head, feet and a very complete and interesting set of internal organs. By the time we got it de-capitated and de-footitated and cleaned (we had a little difficulty there for we weren't quite sure what the organs that the cookbook said must come out, looked like) and stuffed and tied up and had improvised a roasting pan, I wondered more than ever just why I had bought a chicken. I hope that when we eat it we won't still wonder why.

It has been a busy week, but not one in which anything in particular happened. On Monday Blair had a funeral out at Cape Wolfe. And speaking of funerals, the woman who runs the telephone office in O'Leary told him the other day that she would appreciate it if he would preach the sermon he preached at Mrs. So and So's funeral at her funeral. I consider that a real compliment as certainly I have not yet heard a funeral sermon I would like to have at mine (I should note here that I have as yet to hear my husband preach one). The difficulty is that Blair has no idea what sermon he preached at Mrs. So and So's funeral, so we are hoping that nothing will happen to this particular lady until we leave the field.

Tuesday was a very important day because we got the drain of the sink fixed. The job they did on it in the spring was a very temporary one, and unless something more permanent was done before frost got into the ground, we would be using slop pails again all winter. And if that happened we were prepared to just get up and walk out. But on Monday night after supper as I was planning meals for the next day, Blair mentioned casually, By the way, we'll probably have two extra men for both dinner and supper tomorrow! The three of t

(At this point the typewriter broke down, and the letter had to wait until the mechanic in the family had finished his three sermons for the day. It is now Oct. 31st)
Anyway—to continue, the three of them worked all day, and now the drain should work all winter.

On Wednesday it rained all day and Blair got some of that wood piled—but there is still lots of it yet to do.

Friday was our big day for we went to O'Leary and stayed there all day. Blair got the antifreeze put in the car in the morning while I stayed at the Dicksons. Then in the afternoon I went to the doctor—my last visit until that fateful night or day when we knock at his door to tell him that we are on our way to Summerside! Mabel Dickson and I went shopping and practically bought out the drug store there and came home laden with baby powder and baby oil and bottles and nipples and numerous other essentials. And then I blew myself to a shampoo and wave at the O'Leary Beauty Salon. I figured that it was about time that something was done about my hair as I had not washed it since I had left Sydney and that was some time ago. Now I am revelling in the luxury of clean hair. We stayed at Dicksons for supper, too, two meals out in one day was wonderful for us—I don't know whether it was quite as wonderful for the Dicksons.

I can now report that the chicken mentioned in the first paragraph was excellent. Tender and young and juicy and very expertly cooked. We will be getting used to that chicken in the days that lie ahead. Blair was not very keen on the idea of a chicken dinner on Sunday as he would just as soon have something lighter and he said, Now if instead of Sunday we were having chicken dinner on Monday it will be great. To which I replied, "Don't worry, you will be—and Tuesday and Wednesday and Thursday too."

My husband has to go to O'Leary and he is hanging over me waiting for me to get this finished, so I will sign off. This is a terrible letter. Better next week—IF I am still here.

Love,

Joan

In front of the lilac bush

Blair and Michael

Michael in the kindling

Dear Folks,

Surprise, surprise—we're here again! This is the lazy man's way of getting correspondence done, but it really is convenient, so I have decided to start it again for this year. And I see on looking back over past letters that it is just exactly a year ago tonight that I typed my first letter to you—how very much has happened since then—for instance, today is also Michael's birthday, two months old. That bride and groom would never have believed what an awfully sweet thing they were going to produce—and so soon!

Tonight the Colbornes are sitting at home—I am busy here in the kitchen, Blair is in the study and Michael is kicking and gurgling in his carriage in the dining room. Outside the snow is drifting and drifting as the wind sweeps over the Island. We have been having the most awful weather—since Christmas the mailman has missed more days than he did all last year. First of all we had such mild weather that all our roads were a sea of mud, worse than any last spring, and these periods of thawing were followed by quick freezes, which meant roads so rutty and bumpy that the insides were just about shaken out of the car. And now winter has come with a vengeance—I guess all the rest of you had it as well. Blair started out for church on Sunday morning, walking—but it was below zero and the wind was forty miles an hour and at the second fence from us he decided that no one would be fool enough to come to church in such weather—including the minister. So he came home and got all dressed up in his new winter clothes, for what better day would there ever be to find out if they were warm enough. He certainly looked interesting—huge flying suit with fur collar, immense fur gauntlets and his big fur hat and snow boots; so he went for a walk to test them—the only complaint was that they were a bit too warm!

We had thought that our worst complaint about this weather would be the lack of mail, both incoming and outgoing, but this week a new difficulty arose in that Mr. Wilkinson's mother died and the store here was closed right from Saturday night until Thursday morning—and me without any bread. So on Tuesday morning Blair and Alvin Rix went into O'Leary by horse and sleigh and brought back much needed supplies.

Luckily Blair got all his annual meetings over last week before the winter weather began. He had to walk to the one at Cape Wolfe and the one at Bethel, but I guess that didn't hurt him. The churches had done much better financially than we had expected, they had raised all their local expenses and just about all the Mission and Maintenance which both had been upped this year. We were relieved, as it means that we will get 100% of our salary (eventually) which I had completely given up hope of doing.

People have been very good to us. I guess I told you that we were sent a chicken for Christmas—then just as we were finished that Alvin Rix brought us a liver, a huge thing—we have had three liver dinners so far, and I fear that there is still enough there for three more. It is beautiful liver, almost calves, but liver is something that I can take only so much of. Then one of the men from Glenwood came in the other evening and brought us two dozen fresh eggs and two cans of chicken. The eggs were simply a godsend with the store closed and all. I had quite an experience with the gift chicken. When it arrived I saw with great rejoicing that it seemed to be cleaned, so I went ahead and stuffed it and with great labour sewed it all up and put it in the pan. Enter friend husband, always interested in what is going on in the kitchen—"Well, was it well cleaned?" Uh-uh, say I, evading the question. But no, he will not be put off that easily. "Well, was there anything left in it?" Oh I don't think so, say I. "Didn't you even look, didn't you wash it out?" I hated him at that moment, because I realized that I couldn't face eating a bird when we weren't <u>sure</u> that all his organs were removed. So in rage I turned and un-sewed the chicken and took out every bit of stuffing. If the animal was really clean I was about ready to leave him—but no, I discovered lungs and kidneys and wind pipes and sundry things (in fact, the crop may never have come out—after I got the bird sewed up again he asked me about the crop, and even as I realized that I didn't have the foggiest idea whether it was in or out, I said with absolute certainty in my voice, "there is no crop there" and thrust the bird into the oven). Ah well, as Budge says, these things are sent to try us.

I wish so often that you could all see Michael—because he gets cuter all the time. He has begun to laugh now and his hair is coming up in a funny fuzzy little crew cut (it seems to be fair, but it is a little early to tell and he has the most <u>wondering</u> eyes with those long, long lashes, and he almost always sleeps through his 2.00 a.m. feeding now—so you can see that he is daily becoming more and more wonderful. At night these cold times he sleeps with his new little blue kimomo and his white mittens on. He is still so good that I almost worry about him, he will lie awake for hours at a time, never saying a word, although I swear that sometimes he is trying his hardest to talk to us. He weighs, as of last Monday, eleven pounds and six ounces.

Blair has been very busy these days in the study. He found a little stove in the barn and set it up, and is now clearing out the place, then we are going to move a couple of the comfortable chairs from the kitchen in there and we will sit there in the evenings as it is not so drafty as the kitchen and the livingroom. It is going to make a very nice room. But what a job he has to get it cleared up!

Well the first milestone of our married life is passed—I started our first anniversary at three thirty in the morning when I fed the baby. Blair started it a little later as he made the porridge and the coffee and brought in wood and pumped up the water and tramped over to Collicutts for the milk and stirred up the furnace. We both decided that it had been a <u>very</u> good idea!

This is all for our first letter of 1950—these may not be too regular this year, it may be the mailman, it may be just too many diapers to wash—but we love you all just the same ...

```
                              O'Leary R.R.  1
                              P.E.I.
                                 Jan.  22,  1950
```

Hello There,

It's a good bit over a week this time, but anyway, here we are again—at least Michael and I are here, Blair is in church. It is a remarkable day in that all the roads to all the churches have been plowed and are definitely car roads—it probably won't happen again this winter. But for the second week in succession the car has been too cold to go of its own accord, so poor faithful Verne Collicutt has had to tow the minister out of the yard and on the way to church. Verne doesn't go to church himself, but there aren't many people in the community who start our car for church more often.

Last Sunday the roads weren't very good, Blair got to Cape Wolfe all right but the evening service was at Glenwood, so he took the car a certain distance and then walked the rest, about two and a half miles, part of it through pretty deep snow. It was eleven by the time he got home, and he had started at quarter to six—and boy, was he a wreck when he staggered in.

News is rather scarce—mainly we have been interested in the weather, because it has been very, very cold. Ten below won't sound much to some of you people who have been in Winnipeg's 30 below climate, but when you get that wind blowing HARD right across the sea with nothing in its way, it seems mighty cold around here. I have worn slacks for so long that I wouldn't recognize myself if I saw me in a skirt. The new little stove in the study is proving a great blessing, Blair lights it each morning and it warms up the study and diningroom quick as a wink and means that there are no cold drafts in the kitchen. Really only the upstairs is cold, and now that I don't have to get up in the middle of the night to feed Michael, we don't mind that.

But the most serious aspect of this cold weather is what happened to our pipes—and of course it happened on Saturday, which is the day that everything happens to ministers. Yesterday we got up and the pump wouldn't work and neither tap would run. So we spent the day waterless (we felt almost as though we were living in New York although there were a few minor differences), and Oh dear, how very many things there are which you need water for. And Blair spent the day with the pump. At about four o'clock the pump started but there was only water in the bathroom, both pipes downstairs were still frozen. I was able to do my daily diapering in the basin upstairs. It was eight o'clock when Blair, having stood for hours holding a candle to the pipes in the cellar finally unstuck it—Joy Undescribable! But wonder of wonders, the drain did not freeze, that was what I had been dreading, with all the water I use this winter, slop pails would be just too much.

Michael has a new bath tub. With some Christmas money we sent to Simpsons for one of those folding rubber tubs on a stand. It came on Thursday and we were dying to use it F—no, it came Friday and we were going to use it Saturday, but what use is a nice big bath tub without water. So Michael had a sponge bath in just about a saucer. However today while Blair was at his afternoon service I tried it out, and it really seems grand. I can't quite be sure whether or not he likes it or not, because I did an unforgivable thing which rather spoiled the "tone" of our bath hour—namely, I got soap in his eyes, and was he hurt, and <u>mad</u>, he screamed and yelled and roared. Tomorrow we will try again. And tomorrow I will remember that the outlet tube for the water should be hung up on a little hook provided for same, and then I won't have a huge puddle on the floor when the bath is over.

Michael got another present this week. The Bethel Ladies Aid gave him a dear little silver mug with "Michael" (anyway, his name) engraved on it. That was very nice of them, and it makes me forgive them for suddenly calling on me for a "few Words" the last meeting I went to.

Friday was a great day for me—I left my husband to babysit and I went to town. The Collicutts were going and so I seized the opportunity to go along as I had been thinking about getting in to the doctor. I have had two ailments, which while not serious sort of cramped my style. The first was my tongue! I had funny little sores on it and for a day or so I couldn't eat and I couldn't talk, and my, but life was dull! Dr. Dewar gave me some stuff for it and today I feel like a normal tongued creature. Then I had a great big bump on the first finger of my right hand, an infection from—you've guessed it—jabbing myself with a safety pin. I was lucky on that one, The Doctor told me I had just missed having a thing called a "run around" in which the infection runs around the nail and then you have to have your nail removed. But mine didn't run around far enough so he lanced it and today it is all gone. I had a wonderful time in town, I shopped at the drug store, the meat store, the grocery store and the department store and I went to the bank and I saw people and I got news, and I saw a house being moved by twelve horses. I spent a little bit of time at the Dicksons, they are all well. It was a very nice change, and I came home to find my husband with his sleeves rolled up doing dishes—he had prepared formula for Michael and fed him his bottle and Michael was very full and very happy and <u>soaking</u> wet. Blair said that he felt him before he fed him and decided that he would do without changing until I got home.

We are once more avid radio fans, and I give thanks daily for the CBC, it has such wonderful programs of all types. It is truly one thing for which Canadians can be very proud. I wonder if you have heard this new Sunday Evening Hour, a religious period from 8 to 8.45 AST which is the best thing in religious broadcasting I have heard. It comes from Ottawa.

Blair has just come in from church very elated, he not only got a cheque which means we are completely paid up for 1949, but he also preached a <u>good</u> sermon. It was really good too, I read it. I guess it is the result of the study-cleaning operation, he can find his desk and it is more satisfactory to write a sermon at a desk than at the kitchen table.

This is enough for tonight—for a woman who had no news I did pretty well, didn't I?

Love from us all

P.S. Michael weighed twelve pounds a week ago. We forgot to weigh him yesterday when he was <u>ten</u> weeks old.

Dear People,

Look, it's January twenty-ninth! Nearly February. This winter is actually speeding along, I guess it is because I am so busy and Michael is growing and changing so quickly—We just haven't the time to sit and wait for the winter to pass. I let Michael's laundry go for two days last week, and then found myself faced with nineteen diapers and a great array of other miscellaneous stuff. Time sure doesn't hang heavily on my hands.

Michael is starting his thirteenth week of life today and we weighed him yesterday and found that he weighed thirteen pounds. If he continues at this rate we are going to have one great big hunk of boy to take on our holidays—Blair says we will have to get a trailer, remember how much stuff we had last year, without him? He got another present this week—the Ladies Aid of the church where I worked in Sarnia sent him a dear little blue bonnet and sweater set, it looked so cute on him that I put it right on him and he wore it to O'Leary. He is beginning to out grow some of his clothes, one of his little jackets I had to discard absolutely, another I have put away for his sister. He isn't a fat baby yet, although he is very adequately covered, but he is very tall. Mabel Dickson couldn't get over the length of him. His only new accomplishment is that of wiggling and squirming with delight (at least I take it for granted that it is delight) when he smiles at us. We still think he is sort of cute, and oh, we wish so much that you could see him.

Blair is at Cape Wolfe now for the evening service—he came back from Glenwood in high spirits, for we got paid for January, and it isn't even over yet! What utter security we will enjoy if this keeps up.

The week since I last wrote has not been a very exciting one, just normal. The weather has been good enough so that the mailman got round every day. In fact the road seemed so good on the limited stretch we could see that we decided to do something we had not done before, go into O'Leary all three of us. I wanted to telephone the folks in

Halifax while I had a chance—and anyway, we kind of had a hankering to go into Dicksons and show off our son. Of course the car would not go. However after Blair had fiddled with it for hours Verne Collicutt came over with his truck and towed us on our way. The road was frightful! Mud and ice and water a foot deep over some parts of it. The water splashed right over the top of the car and you couldn't see a thing out of the window. Michael was unmoved by the awful drive. I took him right to the manse when we finally arrived in O'Leary—we got there at 2.00 and didn't leave until eight, and I was afraid that his good character would be ruined he got so much attention. I was surprised that he knew right away that here were strangers—Mabel took him while I took my coat off and he took one look and his little cleft chin began to quiver. But he soon recovered and was very good—he went through his whole repertoire of accomplishments, he smiled and wiggled and held up his head and gazed at everything and everybody in the room, he sucked his thumb and hiccupped and burped at both ends. They thought he was a most accomplished child! He didn't have a chance to show what excellent lungs he had for every time he showed any inclination to yell Warren would scoop him up and stride around the room with him. I guess he did that whenever their kids cried—I would crown Blair if he did it to Michael. However I needn't worry, Blair has no desire to walk the floor with his son. I talked to Mum on the phone and Blair got the car looked at again (and this morning it went without a tow, so it must have been a more effective looking than the last) and we had supper and then set out for home. The road was still frightful, not so much water, but more slippery. Blair had to get out three times on the way to wipe mud off the headlights. When we finally arrived I decided that I was satisfied to stay put right here for the rest of the winter.

This last week of January is always a troublesome one for ministers, and Blair has been deep in the annual reports, huge blue forms requiring copious information. However now they are finished and in the mail. Now we are thinking of starting a Married Couples Club here and we have issued a general invitation for anyone interested to come here a week from tomorrow night. There is a definite need for something of that sort—we certainly would relish an opportunity to get together with other couples. We're not at all sure how the thing will shape up, a discussion group, or a Farm Radio Forum group, or a social club—but we'll see.

I forgot to tell you in my last letter about the big piece of news round here: Last week in below zero temperature with a gale warning a young couple started out about five in the morning from Cape Wolfe to O'Leary, by horse and sleigh. They got as far as the house past Wilkinson's store, but couldn't go any farther, and a baby boy was born in the Currys' kitchen. I'm sure glad that they didn't stop here—and I'm also very glad that Michael is born and we're not expecting him round now.

Latest reports on who Michael looks like: from the eyes up he is definitely like Dad A., but Myrtle Rix the girl next door, having seen Budge's picture says that he definitely has a look of her. Nobody seems to think he looks like his parents!

Oh, by the way, my finger and my tongue are completely recovered!

I guess that is all for this week . . .

        love to all of you,

O'Leary R. R. 1,
P.E.I.
Feb. 7th

Dear Folks,

Another week has rushed by and now it is Tuesday—somehow Sunday didn't seem to be a letter writing-y sort of day at all. But this being Tuesday evening I will have to rush my writing of this—I must be through before "The Mystery Theatre, with Inspector Hearthstone of the Death Squad" comes on the radio. Blair is a passionate Hearthstone fan so we are not allowed to miss it. I shall therefore have to do the best I can in a limited time.

It has been a cold week with below zero temperatures and high winds, but Blair managed to spend one day in O'Leary and another visiting old ladies down at Cape Wolfe, so there has been some car weather. And the pump only froze once (this morning, when I had three days of baby wash to do!) and it came unthawed very quickly. Michael had to sleep in his blue coat with the hood and Blair and I were very happy to have long sleeved flannel nightgowns (and each other). Sunday was the coldest and most miserable day—as isn't it always and Blair had two awful drives to church—a regular gale blowing and minus temperature and twenty miles in horse and sleigh. Alvin Rix next door drove him and he has a really fast mare, Blair had nearly asked Albert Moorshead of across the road who has two horses that I can walk much faster than— he was certainly glad that he hadn't. For what the well-dressed cleric will wear you really should have seen the Rev. B. B. Colborne setting out for divine service on Sunday. In that flying suit he looked like a member of Operation Muskox—but he wasn't the least bit cold (except his face and I didn't hear about that until Monday when he decided that it was really too sore to shave!)

Tuesday was a red letter day in our lives—we got the new linoleum down in the bedroom, and what a difference it makes! Blair put it down and made a BEAUTIFUL job of it, some of the women who were here last night decided to have him come and lay theirs. I had known that the stuff that was down was old but we hadn't known just how old until we took it up and found newspapers of February 1929—twenty one years ago (for the benefit of anyone whose arithmetic is bad). Reading the papers took valuable labour time but certainly was interesting. 1929 was "Progress Year" in Nova Scotia and the Mail had a special progress edition, everything was booming: King George the V was seriously ill and the Prince of Wales was dashing halfway across the globe to his bedside. Lord Willingdon was Governor General of Canada—and you should see the ads for cars and clothes. It was very entertaining and it is so wonderful to have a new clean shining floor with no holes in it.

Our son continues to be the sweetest baby in the world. We wonder if we are prejudiced. Alvin Rix when he saw him on Sunday commented on just two things about our Michael: 1) what big ears he had and 2) the spot on the back of his head where he is completely bald. But no, we're not prejudiced, he is the sweetest baby we ever saw—at any rate, says Blair, he is the sweetest baby we ever had. He is now the proud possessor of his first pair of diamond socks! His aunt Budge knit them for him in pink and blue and white and they look so cute on his little feet. Four days ago I started him on pablum, his first attempt at semi-solid food—and what a struggle. He howled everytime I tried to give him any and refused to swallow it and kept blocking any access to his mouth with a thumb and a couple of fingers. And at the end of each attempt was just covered with pablum from head to toe. This morning, having decided that likely he would have to be fed on liquids all the rest of his life, I rolled up my sleeves, gritted my teeth and decided to try again. Michael opened his mouth, gobbled down the pablum and swallowed it and waited open mouthed for the next bite. What happened I will never know—but I am glad that it did.

Last night we had visitors—it was the first time in a long while. We issued a general invitation for anyone interested in starting an adult group, as I told you last week. We got all ready for them. I baked and we got the house cleaned up and Blair shaved and I put on my new ear rings which Ed gave me for Christmas and as Blair said, Even if nobody came, it was good for our morale. We had twelve here, all really interested in starting some sort of group, especially during the winter. It will have devotion, discussion, diversion and digestion and will meet here at the manse two Monday evenings a month. We felt it was a worthwhile evening, and now we will see what comes of it.

I have forgotten in my last couple of letters to tell you of another art which Blair had been developing, as well as linoleum laying—he makes superb fudge! Previously I had been the fudge maker of the family but I always had the most rotten luck with it, either it never hardened or else it got so hard that we had to chop it out of the pot. But his is always a perfect consistency. I have made my last fudge.

That seems to be all for now—I must join my husband and Inspector Hearthstone.

with love,

The Manse,
O'Leary RR1,
P.E.I.
Feb. 16, 1950

Dear People,

The snow is snowing, the wind is blowing, and outside the drifts are piling high around our house. It is the worst snow of the year so far, it has never stopped all day and there is more forecast for tomorrow. The drift outside our back door must be nearly five feet by now (and even for me that isn't much exaggeration). No mail tomorrow, I fear—he came today in his little red sleigh and his great fur coat, reminding me of Santa Claus. The trip just over to Collicutts for the mail seems like a long, long trek in this weather.

But enough of the weather, surely there are other things of interest to talk about in the lives of the Colbornes of the Island. Well, my great accomplishment of the week is that I have baked my first batch of bread! Lucky I did too, for if I hadn't we would have had to find our way to the store through the blizzard. Was I ever proud of myself—if we had had all the little bits and pieces of equipment that go with that camera I would have had my photo taken with my first two loaves. It was quite good too.

Then another thing of great importance was that Michael passed another milestone—three months, and we decided that it was about time he graduated out of the nightgown stage into little boy clothes stage. So on his three months birthday I put on the little blue knitted suit that his Grandma C. sent him for Christmas. I wish you could have seen him in it, he was so cute—but I just wanted to burst into tears, for Michael wasn't our little baby any more, he had suddenly become a little boy. But each night when I put on his nightie, I have my baby back. One reason that I was reluctant to put on suits was that we were so short of them but just on time he got a Valentine from his Grandma A., a dear little pink jersey suit, so he is well away. Then I am knitting him a blue two piece suit with yellow ducks swimming across the sweater, but at the rate I am going he will be adolescent before his ducky suit is finished. Now for other news about our son: he weighs, as of Monday, 13 pounds, 10 ounces, he is eating up his pablum and loving his bath, he still has cradle cap and diaper rash and the most <u>peculiar</u> bowels, but he also has the sweetest smile and the cheerfulest disposition and he never wakes until after seven in the morning. We figure that his eyes are going to stay blue, a nice dark blue, and to our amazement his hair of which he still has no great abundance, has a definite reddish glint. And he is just crazy about his father, he won't even eat if can see and grin at his dad. So that's our kid. We're getting kind of fond of him.

It is a long time since we had the car out, Blair went to church by sleigh last Sunday and he very likely will again this week. I hope he will be able to get into O'Leary soon—his hair keeps growing and growing even though we are so far from a barber's.

Last Sunday Myrtle Rix came over to spend the afternoon with me and she brought young Alan, aged three—it gave one a glimpse into the future. Alan never stopped from the time he arrived in the house, and not one thing escaped his notice. I just piled everything breakable on the top of the stove and we went on talking and not taking much notice of him, but I looked around at one point and I had to laugh, for the kitchen was a shambles, on the floor were papers and magazines and the pantry towel, the scrub board was propped beside Myrtle's chair, in the centre of the room was the little stool with four empty coke bottles on it, and as I talked I found that I was holding three sticks of kindling, a coke bottle and an empty maple syrup tin—Myrtle was holding three sticks of kindling, a coke bottle and a mouse trap. Oh dear, I hope that Michael won't do that in other persons' houses, but how are we going to keep him from it.

We have had more visitors in the last little while than we did for a time there, each day someone seems to drop in. A couple of weeks ago during that awfully cold spell we didn't see anyone for so long that I was getting just sick of the sight of my husband and my child. On Monday I went down to the community hall for a Social Evening. It could hardly be classed as one of the most entertaining evenings I have ever spent, but I rather enjoyed a chance to compare notes on <u>my</u> child with other mothers there. Last week was supposed to be Ladies Aid, but the weather was too bad to go. So the CBC is still providing most of our entertainment. After debating it for nearly a year we finally last month subscribed to the CBC Times Weekly so that we get information on radio programs ahead of time and can really choose what we want to hear. Last evening we heard the Vienna Boys Choir and a play, The Importance of Being Earnest by Oscar Wilde. Tonight the big feature was the Citizens Forum discussion of How can we have World Peace?—tomorrow is travel night and quiz night, a trip through Ireland with Prof. Phelps of McGill and Beat the Champs. Sunday is so many things—and of course Tuesday is always Hearthstone of the Death Squad. You can see that our entertainment is varied. The fact that we live in the days of electricity doesn't really mean much to us, but oh, I'm thankful that we don't live in the pre-radio times.

There must be more news, but I can't think of any right now, and I will get this letter ready just in case the mailman should come tomorrow.

Our love to all of you,

Joan

February 24th, 1950

Hello there!

It's over a week since I wrote to you and we have had a series of storms since—in this part of the country winter never seems to come until February is nearly over, but then—oh boy. The state of the weather is indicated by the state of Blair's hair, when we really have a clear spell then he will go to O'Leary and get a haircut, and nobody round here will recognize him. We had a storm on Monday and a storm on Wednesday and another on Thursday and by this morning we had to practically dig our way out—inside the shut door of the woodshed the snow drifts were three feet high. We have winter tenants, a group of twelve partridges are camping on our property, each morning when we come down we see that somewhere close to the house out of the wind there is a round hole about a foot deep dug right down under the crust of snow where they all huddle together in a little tight ball. I am under no illusions this year as I was last that the end of February marks the beginning of spring—I haven't seen a single trace of that wonderful season yet.

For the first time this winter Blair and I both had colds this last week, neither of them very bad, luckily. Blair tried this anti-histamine drug and he says he thinks it helped him. By the time I got round to catching the cold the store here was out of the tablets so I didn't have an opportunity to judge their effectiveness. We're both over the cold now and as yet there is no sign of Michael getting it. I was worried that he would so I wore a mask whenever I changed or fed him. He seems to be a pretty healthy young critter. Fourteen pounds, two ounces he weighed last Saturday—and he is so long that he is outgrowing his carriage.

Michael is still kind of cute. His latest accomplishment is eating apple sauce. I started him on it last week and there were none of the struggles that were involved in pablum, he laps up his apple sauce pronto. And he has made another great stride forward in his development— he has discovered that he has a hand (I don't think he realizes yet that he has <u>two</u> hands, what a great day that will be!) and it fascinates him. He lies for hours on his back with one arm stretched straight up in the air and just looks at this very remarkable hand he has discovered. He has discovered none of the amazing uses this hard has, he simply knows that it is there.

We have become amateur photographers. After much letter writing and parcel sending between Sydney, Halifax and the Island we have assembled (thanks to Ed) all the equipment necessary to get pictures of Michael. Blair has mentally digested volumes of directions and instructions, and last night we put on Michael's best sweater and put him on his tummy on his bath table and took a couple of flash pictures of him. We're sending that roll of film off tomorrow, and we can't wait to see it.

Today was the World Day of Prayer for Women and the service was held at Bethel church. I had to speak at the service and I walked thru huge snowdrifts and was quite worn out when got there. It was a lovely day though, sunny and although it was windy it wasn't cold. Our prayer meeting was not large, there were just six of us, and two of these were men! At our world day of prayer meeting we always close by eating copiously, which is a pleasant custom. I got a sleighride home and a dozen doughnuts and half a chocolate cake.

Sunday. Blair said I did not finish this on Friday night as there would be no mail on Saturday. And there certainly wasn't. One sleigh went by at about nine on Sat. morning, but not one other living creature or any vehicle went by. The snow had piled up deep overnight and went on snowing and drifting all day. Today dawned, a lovely sunny day, but Blair was to go to Cape Wolfe this morning with Ray Collicutt, and Ray said that it was too bad driving to attempt it, the snow is so very deep and heavy that it would just about kill a horse. He (Blair) walked to Bethel this afternoon but no one came, and the Glenwood people called and said that they were not expecting him. So it has been a very queer Sunday with my husband around all day. But kind of nice.

We have been living high all week. Which simply means that we have been eating meat not out of cans. One of the people at Glenwood gave Blair a big round steak roast and a piece of pork last Sunday—it came at a time when we were so utterly sick of canned meat that we wanted to scream. And after all the snow this weekend, I don't know when we will ever get to town to get meat—Ray Collicutt says that now he doesn't expect to see his car until spring, but the drift down his driveway is <u>a little</u> deeper than ours.

As always I have said to Blair, Now, what else should I say in my letter? He grunted and said, Tell them what a nice husband you have! So I will—I have a very nice husband. He did a big wash for me on Friday—I discovered that he had all his life wanted to do a laundry! It made me feel quite guilty for a week or so before I got quite fed up with having him under foot in the kitchen all the time, so I just put my foot down and said that the kitchen was my domain and he could darn well stay in his study unless invited in. But even in our isolated situation here everybody knows what you are doing—yesterday he went to the store and one of the men who lives next to the store said, We see that you are spending a lot more time in your study lately! Likely everybody thinks we have had a big fight. Anyway we are still friends.

That is all for now—we haven't seen the mailman since Thursday and I don't know when we will, but at least this will be ready to go.

with love,

Joan

The Manse,
The Island,
March 4th

Hello Again,

It is March 4th, the temperature this morning was fourteen below, the pipes and the pump froze during the night, for over a week, eleven days, our only contact with O'Leary and civilization has been a single track sleigh trail and some days not even that. In fact it doesn't seem one bit springlike round here. And yet there must be a faint breath of spring somewhere somehow, for I find within me a great surging desire to start spring cleaning! This may not be due to the approach of spring—it may be just the filth of the house. On Monday I paid a visit to our nextdoor neighbor and she said that she too was just itching to get started cleaning, so it may be the first faint sign of spring.

About half an hour ago we were sitting in the kitchen, the dishes were done, the baby fed and the sun had just gone down. I was looking down the road when it happened—I heard a car, then I realized that at last I was getting "bushed", even beginning to hear things. But when I looked at Blair I realized that he was thinking exactly the same thing, then, to our great relief the snow plow hove into sight, making a noise just like a car! It was nice to have the plow through, and it was also nice to know that in spite of a week of not having been anywhere or done anything or seen anyone but us we have <u>not</u> yet begun hearing sounds that are not there.

My remark that we had not been anywhere is not absolutely correct. Blair certainly went places on Wednesday. It was just about the worst day all year, a regular blizzard and drifting snow—and there was a funeral, at the very uttermost end of the field. They decided at the last minute to hold the funeral in Cape Wolfe church. Ray Collicutt took Blair and they had a terrific drive, part of the way they had to break the road and the trail kept drifting in. Another foot of snow on some of the drifts and they said that the horse would not have been able to get through at all.

But in spite of all there have been some perfectly beautiful days, cold, clear, bright and crisp, when you just feel as though winter is the best month of the year. Monday and Tuesday were such days and I got out and went visiting and to the store and just came back feeling wonderful. The time of the full moon is here and the nights are just magnificent, the sky is filled with stars and it is nearly as light as day.

We are making strides ahead in culinary arts. This week I made doughnuts for the first time. But the real shocking event of the week took place on Monday when the minister went to work in the kitchen and <u>all on his own</u> baked a batch of the most beautiful whole wheat bread that I have ever tasted. It was golden brown and a perfect texture—he just wanted to see if he could do it. Sometimes I am inclined to think that maybe we should trade jobs—or perhaps trade them month about.

Dear me, that seems to be all that went on this week—Michael continues to grow, so does Blair's hair—but this letter is about to stop....

With love from your very snowed in
children,

our only contact with O'Leary and civilization has be
k sleigh trail and some days not even that. In fact i
bit springlike round here. And yet there must be a fa
ng somewhere somehow, for I find within me a great sur
t spring cleaning! This may not be due to the approach
may be just the <u>filth</u> fo the house. On Monday I paid a
door neighbor and she said that she too was just itchi
ted cleaning, so it may be the first faint sign of spr

About half an hour ago we were sitting in the kitchen
done, the baby fed and the sun had just gone down. I
the road when it happened --I heard a car, then I rea
I was getting "bushed", even beginning to hear things
ked at Blair I realized that he was thinking exactly th
, to our great relief the snow plow hove into sight, m
like a car! It was nice to have the plow through, an
to know that in spite of a week of not having been an
thing or seen anyone but us we have <u>not</u> yet begun heari
not there.

My remark that we had not been anywhere is not absolu
r certainly went places on Wednesday. It was just abo
year, a regular blizzard and drifting snow - and ther
he very uttermost end of the field. They decided at t
old the funeral in Cape Wolfe church. Ray Collicutt t
had a terrific drive, part of the way they had to bre
trail kept drifting in. Another foot of snow on some o
they said that the horse would not have been able to g

But in spite of all there have been some perfectly be
, clear, bright and crisp, when you just feel as thoug
best month of the year. Monday and Tuesday were such d
and went visiting and to the store and just came back
The time of the full moon is here and the nights are
t, the sky is filled with stars and it is nearly as li

We are making strides ahead in culinary arts. This w
hnuts for the first time. But the real cooking event
place on Monday when the minister went to work in the
<u>on his own</u> baked a batch of the most beautiful whole w
I have ever tasted. It was golden brown and a perfec
just wanted to see if he could do it. Sometimes I am i
k that maybe we should trade jobs - or perhaps take th

Dear me, that seems to be all that went on this week
inues to grow, so does Blair's hair - but this letter
. . .

With love from your very snowed in children,

Epilogue

Mum and Michael today

the manse today

Joan Archibald Colborne

Epilogue

Whenever I have shown these letters to anyone, the reaction has always been the same: "What about the baby? All of a sudden he's there and you don't tell us anything about his arrival!"

So let me tell you about that awesome day. Our baby was due November 12, 1950. We were to have it (the gender of an unborn child in those days being an unfathomable mystery) in Summerside at Prince County Hospital, about fifty miles away. November 12th just felt like an ordinary day until we got a phone call on our party line from my parents: they had arrived from Ottawa to Summerside to await the birth. I was furious! They would stay until the baby was born—and I had nothing in the house to eat. I made ginger cookies, but, as the last batch came out of the oven, I felt my first labour pain (we had pains then, we didn't know that they were only contractions).

We set off for Summerside right away—and our Catholic car behaved beautifully, and we arrived at the hospital where Blair let me off (in those days the husband had no place by his wife in the delivery room). He went to the hotel to meet my parents, and during supper Michael Blair Colborne was born. On November 12th—just as he was supposed to be. I thought I would burst with love. It was an epiphany.

My letters from then on became much less regular. I discovered that a baby can take up a great deal of time and work. Disposable diapers were unknown, and, with a washtub and a scrub board, it was very slow work. The diapers were hung up every day—except Sunday—on the clothesline, and mine were always two or three hours appearing after everyone else's. I decided that I had to do the diapers on Sunday, too, or I couldn't manage on Monday, so I cheated. I hung my wash in an empty bedroom. One beautiful sunny Sunday I hung out my wash anyway—and to my amazement all the neighbours' washes were hung out within half an hour. It was the first evidence I had of the influence of the minister's wife in a commmunity.

Readers will notice that I didn't write much about summer on the Island. I'm sorry, but as soon as summer started, I left, and went back home to Nova Scotia. The women in the community were beginning to plan for the big summer undertaking: a turkey supper to which every woman was expected to make six pies—and I had never made one—so I just took off. And PEI then was not the touristy holiday haven it is now. So I went to visit my parents on the south shore of Nova Scotia.

I was not very young—twenty-six, I had two degrees, I had a nice trousseau so I was better-dressed than I have ever been before or since—but I have never in my life felt so inept in that community. I couldn't manage to wash lamp chimneys until they shone. I couldn't manage to wax my linoleum floors till they shone. I had never washed a man's shirt before I set foot on the Island—and then I had to iron it with a flat iron—and poor Blair never looked nice and crisp. I couldn't invite the Ladies Aid to the Manse until I had learned to bake five different kinds of sweets, because they had a rule that the hostess must serve no more than five different sweets.

The women of Springfield West did all these things so easily and so well. They also worked in the fields, they milked cows, and dug potatoes. How those women worked!

Blair and I felt we were lucky. Almost all the young couples had to live with their parents or in-laws. We were given a free furnished house—sometimes furnished with leftovers from members of the Congregation—but we had something that nobody else our age had: a house of our own. It may have been shabby and the kitchen drain didn't work. And we never would have chosen the furniture, and we had rats—but it was all ours for as long as we lived in it.

When I look at my life now, I think that what I would miss most is my refrigerator. We kept food on the steps going down to the cellar. It wasn't very efficient, but it was what everyone did. There was only one refrigerator in the community. It ran on gas and belonged to the storekeeper who was considered to be the most affluent person in Springfield West.

But it was not a lack of refrigerator or washing machine that bothered me most—it was that nobody except my husband ever called me by my first name. And it is lonely to be treated with so much respect.

In 1951, Blair, Michael, and I left Springfield West and moved to Halifax, where Blair was appointed General Secretary of the Student Christian Movement at Dalhousie University. We had electric lights and a washing machine and an upstairs apartment in the city, and everyone called me by my first name!

During our two years in Halifax, we had a daughter, Ann. We returned to rural life in 1953, to Milford Station, a village near Truro. Our second son, David, was born while we lived there. Three years later we moved our growing family to Shelburne, a small town on the South Shore of Nova Scotia. Blair loved this church and its congregation, and we stayed there for eleven years. Twin daughters, Heather and Janet, were born there.

The role of the minister's wife is very different today. In those days I guess the minister and his wife were considered very important people in the community. Ministers' wives did not work— for money. I started to teach school when Michael was in Grade 12, and we had been in Shelburne for ten years—and I said to Blair, "Do you suppose the Congregation will mind?" Always you wondered if the Congregation would mind.

In 1967, we moved to Rockingham, on the outskirts of Halifax, where I completed my Bachelor of Education at Mount Saint Vincent University. I taught elementary school in Rockingham until 1976, when we moved to Hampton, New Brunswick. By this time all five children had left home, and I continued teaching in Hampton and Quispamsis until my retirement in 1988 at age 65. Blair died in Hampton in 1980, at the age of 54. I continue to live in Hampton. Although a stroke in 1992 slowed me down, I remain actively involved with my friends, my church, and my family.

I have eleven grandchildren and two great-grandchildren who live in Canada, England, South Africa, and the United States.

And it all started in that manse on the Island.

129 Joan Archibald Colborne

Joan Archibald Colborne was born in Halifax, the daughter of lawyer and judge Maynard B. Archibald, and Helen Dustan, who was a descendant of the pioneer clergyman Rev. James MacGregor. A graduate of Dalhousie University, Joan attended the United Church Training School in Toronto, worked as a Secretary in the Student Christian Movement at the University of Saskatchewan, and was a lay minister in Sarnia, Ontario. She married the newly ordained Rev. Blair Colborne in Ottawa in 1948, and immediately moved to Prince Edward Island, where she wrote these letters.

In 1952 Joan and Blair were transferred to Halifax. They went on to raise five children, and lived in Milford Station, Shelburne, and Rockingham, where she completed her Bachelor of Education at Mount Saint Vincent University and taught elementary school. In 1976, they settled in Hampton, New Brunswick, where Joan continued to teach and participate in United Church women's issues until she retired in 1985. She remains actively involved with friends, church, and family.